# The Race of Time

# The race of Time

*three lectures
on Renaissance
historiography
by
Herschel Baker*

University of Toronto Press

©University of Toronto Press 1967
Printed in U.S.A.
Library of Congress Catalog Card No. 66-29031

*How soon hath thy prediction, seer blest,*
*Measured this transient world, the race of time,*
*Till time stand fixed: beyond is all abyss,*
*Eternity, whose end no eye can reach.*

Paradise Lost, *XII.553-556*

For Douglas Bush

The Alexander Lectureship was founded in honor of Professor W. J. Alexander, who held the Chair of English at University College, University of Toronto, from 1889 to 1926. Each year the Lectureship brings to the University a distinguished scholar or critic to give a course of lectures on a subject related to English literature.

# Preface

It is pleasant to recall the circumstances under which I gave these Alexander Lectures at the University of Toronto in the fall of 1965 and to remember the generous hospitality of Principal Douglas LePan, Professor Clifford Leech, and their colleagues in University College.

Since the lectures are here printed in their original form, in an effort to keep the documentation of a massive subject within reasonable limits, I have in all but one or two instances confined myself to primary sources. I have modernized titles in the lectures, but not in the notes; and except for rendering indiscriminate italics as roman, bringing *i—j* and *u—v* into conformity with modern orthography, and silently expanding nasal contractions (*commō-common*), I have tried to reproduce the often capricious texts as accurately as human frailty permits.

The dedication of this little book – to a most distinguished alumnus of the University of Toronto – is a small expression of my large affection and esteem for one who for many years has been my teacher, friend, and colleague. No scholar of his time has served his calling better.

H.B.

*Harvard University*
*7 December 1965*

# Contents

# the Truth
# of history

History, as a form of writing, was esteemed so highly in the English Renaissance that Sir Philip Sidney's comments on the subject almost take us by surprise. To be sure, he was not so blunt as Doctor Johnson, who deplored the historian's "shallow stream of thought" and compared his talent for "reflection" to a cat's when she is about to seize a mouse,[1] but he viewed the subject with urbane contempt, and in *An Apology for Poetry* its spokesman is depicted as an object of derision. Pompous and assertive, this man is shown to be a fusty pedant "loden with old Mouse-eaten records . . . , a wonder to young folkes and a tyrant in table talke," who quotes Cicero to document his ample self-esteem and who denies, "in a great chafe, that any man for teaching of vertue, and vertuous actions, is comparable to him." In Sidney's view this buffoon is crippled by his own absurd pretensions. For one thing, his vaunted erudition, which is mainly built on plagiarism and on "the notable foundation of Heare-say," embalms the partial truth and privileged error; for another, his boast of teaching virtue by example is invalidated by his own procedures, for he is "so tyed," says Sidney, "not to what shoulde bee but to what is, to the particuler truth of things and not to the general reason of things," that his knowledge can exert no moral force.[2]

I cite this famous passage not because it represents

the standard view, but because it expresses, even for a hostile purpose, a pair of ancient commonplaces that underlie most Renaissance discussions of historiography. One is that the historian, unlike other writers, has a special obligation to ascertain and state the truth of things. The other is that such truths are exemplary: they are paradigms of moral and political behavior, which, authenticated by famous men's experience, provide patterns that can shape our own response to perennially recurring situations. Thus history, unlike more imaginative kinds of literature, was thought to be both true and useful. It had a dual sanction, and generations of humanists, politicians, and moralists – who by no means represented mutually exclusive categories – concurred in celebrating it. For such men, history was, as one of them explained,

the marrow of reason, the creame of experience, the sap of wisdome, the pith of judgement, the librarie of knowledge, the kernell of policie, the unfoldresse of treacherie, the kalendar of time, the lanterne of truth, the life of memorie, the doctresse of behaviour, the register of antiquitie, the trumpet of chivalrie.[3]

But if truth and utility were the slogans of conventional historians long before and after Sidney derogated them, his strictures serve a useful purpose in posing as they do some fundamental questions, for in a sense they inaugurated a continuing reappraisal of the aims and methods of historiography that ran throughout the later Renaissance in England. To be sure, this reappraisal was anything but neat and systematic. We must remember that the legendary history of Britain, with its fantastic tales of Trojan Brut and his descendants, was purveyed as fact long after it had been rejected by the soundest scholars of the age; that concurrently with such avant-garde works as

Selden's *History of Tithes* (1618) and Bacon's life of Henry VII (1622), John Speed massively perpetuated the chronicle tradition of Grafton, Hall, and Holinshed with his *History of Great Britain* (1611), a folio that reached its fourth edition in 1650 and that was re-issued, in a shorter form, a generation later; that the civil war was already under way when Sir Richard Baker published, in 1643, the immensely popular *Chronicle of the Kings of England* which Addison and Fielding would urbanely ridicule; that just when Hobbes was completing his *Leviathan* the learned Bishop Ussher dated the creation of the world as shortly before midnight on Monday, October 23, 4004 B.C. Polydore Vergil in the early Tudor period and Sir Walter Raleigh about a century later remind us that there were anticipations and survivals which baffle easy formulation, that old and new ideas were often juxtaposed, and that sometimes they were tangled in a web which cannot be unsnarled. None the less, the six decades separating the publication of Camden's *Britannia* in 1586 and the start of Clarendon's work on *The History of the Rebellion* were productive not only of a staggering bulk of historical writing in both prose and verse but also of a gradual transformation in the historian's own conception of his function and procedures. It will be the business of these lectures to examine some of the anticipations and survivals in Renaissance historiography and to glance at some of their effects in literature.

▢ It may be useful to begin by reconstructing, if we can, those basic Renaissance opinions about historiography that prompted Sidney's disrespect and that, despite progressive modification, retained a certain vitality as late as Milton's day. By then, some of these commonplaces, which were as old at least as Cicero, had dwindled into slogans whose persistent popularity certified little more than the force of incremental repetition, but they none the less remained the refuge of historians; they codified the Renaissance ideal; and, as we shall see, they continued to define the limits of discussion even though their meaning was being drained away.

The first of these received opinions was that historians, as opposed to other kinds of writers, were distinguished by their deep commitment to the truth. This truth was rarely well defined, and often not defined at all, but almost all historians talked about it with more or less familiarity, and many of them used it as their shield and buckler. Poets like Sidney and Donne might ridicule those plodding searchers after fact who, ignoring "the general reason of things," were so intent on "What Caesar did, yea, and what Cicero said"[4] that they never reached the higher realm of spirit, but the Renaissance historian was complacent with and even boastful of his limitations. After all, Cicero had declared veracity to be the first law of history;[5] Quintilian had defined it as an exposition of the actual truth of things (*gestae rei expositio*), whose force is equal to its candor;[6] and even the most partisan and mendacious of chroniclers could take shelter in their great prestige. Therefore when Sidney's fatuous historian quoted – or rather misquoted – Cicero to secure his title as *lux veritatis* he merely echoed (and anticipated) countless of his fellows.[7]

Thus a pedagogue like Roger Ascham, fired by reading Livy, thought that to "write nothyng false" was the first requirement of historians.[8] In the same vein Thomas Cooper, whose many achievements as scholar and ecclesiastic included an influential chronicle, a famous Latin-English dictionary, and the bishopric of Winchester, said that it was the historian's high distinction to correct the distortions and evasions of small-minded men in order to assert the painful truth – "the ambicion of Caesar, the drunkennesse of Tyberius, the pryde of Caligula, the crueltee of Nero, the vicious lyfe of Heliogabalus."[9] John Knox expressed the hope that "discreet" readers of his savagely partisan *History of the Reformation in Scotland* would endorse his record of the "simple truth."[10] In a eulogistic preface to Grafton's *Chronicle at Large* (1569) Thomas Norton – the translator of Calvin's *Institutes* and co-author of *Gorboduc* – declared that any reader of this "large, playne, true, and meere" history of the realm could be "certified of truth."[11] Thomas Blundeville, a retainer of the Earl of Leicester whose *True Order and Method of Writing and Reading Histories* (1574) is a conflation of two influential Italian treatises, distinguished "Philosophers and Hystoriographers" from poets by their desire "to tell things as they were done without either augmenting or diminishing them, or swarving one jote from the truth."[12] Jean Bodin, the profoundest student of historiography of the sixteenth century, called those readers "stupid" who looked for literary effects when they should be looking for the truth. "I have made up my mind," he said, "that it is practically an impossibility for the man who writes to give pleasure, to impart the truth of the matter also – a thing which Thucydides, Plutarch, and Diodorus criticized in Herodotus. I wonder why Cicero called him the father of history, when all antiquity accuses him of falsehood."[13] Johannes Sleiden, whose great history of the Reformation (1555) remains a monument to his scholarship and zeal, declared that truth and candor were "the two most becoming Ornaments of an History" and that it had been his "utmost care" to exemplify these virtues. "To that end I have taken up nothing upon surmise or light report," he said, "but I have studiously collected what I have here written from the Publick Records and Papers; the faith of which can justly be call'd in question by no man."[14] Speaking of his annals of Elizabeth, Camden explained that just as "the love of Truth" had been his only motive in undertaking such immense exertions, it had also been his "onely Scope and Aim." For to take away the truth from history, he went on to say, "is nothing else but, as it were, to pluck out the Eyes of the beautifullest Creature in the World; and, instead of wholesome Liquor, to offer a Draught of Poison to the Readers Minds."[15] There can be no doubt that the man who dedicated his book "To God, my Country and Posterity, at the Altar of Truth"[16] would regard the tribute of his former student as the highest accolade: "What name, what skill, what faith hast thou in things!" said Jonson of his honored master.[17]

And so the testimony mounts as one generation of historians is succeeded by another. Daniel, whose failure to complete *The Civil Wars* no doubt showed his discontent with verse as a medium for historical narration, vowed as a writer of prose history "to bee of no other side, then of Truth, or as neere truth-likelinesse as I possibly can get."[18] This was also Bacon's aim in his life of Henry VII, as he bluntly told Prince Charles: "I have not flattered him, but took him to life as well as I could, sitting so far off, and having no better light."[19] The fabulously learned Selden said that he wrote his *History of Tithes* – a very ticklish subject – to provide an "Armorie" for those who, "preferring Truth before what dulling custom hath too deeply rooted in them, are not unwilling to change their old akorns for better meat." He had, as he conceded, perhaps offended orthodox opinion; but his conclusions had been built on demonstrated fact: his goal had been the "Sanctuarie of Truth," not the "base court of her Temple" where "common Opinion and vulgar suppositions" are content to dwell.[20] Whatever the difficulties of reconstructing "the abstruse condition of causes, counsels, facts, and their circumstances," said Edmund Bolton about his own researches on the Emperor Nero, the effort was essential, for "howsoever lights may faile, yet truth is the supreme aime of every right narrationer."[21] Launching his *Life and Reign of King Henry the Eighth* (1649), Lord Herbert of Cherbury felt armed against the hostile critics of his book. "I shall little care for censure," he declared, "as long as the testimonies I use doe assure and warrant me: since I intend not to describe him otherwise, either good or bad, but as He really was."[22] A few years later, when the cantankerous Peter Heylin came to write his *Ecclesia Restaurata; or, the History of the Reformation of the Church of England* (1661), he too professed complete detachment in dealing with a controversial subject. Why rub ointment on a tumor that needs lancing, he inquired. "For in this case a true historian must have somewhat in him of the good Samaritan, in using wine or vinegar, to cleanse the wound, as well as oil, to qualify the grief of the inflammation."[23]

To end this catalogue of witnesses, which could be indefinitely expanded, we may cite the second English poet, for it is he who most eloquently and even arrogantly proclaims the ancient prerogatives of the real historian as spokesman for the truth. Milton's scorn for those "obscure and blockish chronicles" where the "fables and impertinences" of ignorant monks were used to hide the facts and support a wicked cause[24] is counterpointed by soaring commendation of the history that relies on naked truth. It is this kind of history that the real hero deserves, he said, for by its "immortal record his noble deeds, which else were transitory, become fixed and durable against the force of years and generations, [and] he fails not to continue through all posterity, over Envy, Death, and Time also victorious."[25]

□ If these ardent testimonials, which cut across most shades of the political and theological opinion of eight decades or so, seem to point to a remarkable unanimity about the historian's high resolve to state the truth of things, they by no means indicate agreement as to the nature of this truth or the means by which it is attained. This fact is really not surprising, for in an age of such incessant altercation there were many kinds of truth, and no man could accommodate them all. Indeed, one contemporary of Milton's, who recognized his own restrictions, launched a gigantic survey of things in general by announcing at the start that he wrote not only as a scholar but also as an Englishman, and not only as an Englishman but – "which is somewhat more" – as a churchman of the Church of England.[26] Such candor is refreshing, for labels like

Catholic and Protestant, royalist and parliamentarian, Anglican and Puritan denoted not only convictions and beliefs, but also attitudes, assumptions, and configurations of opinion that were bound to shape a man's perception and thus his presentation of the so-called facts. Depending on his point of view, such facts would seem to bear their own credentials, or they would seem to be not merely wrong but evil. For example, Johannes Sleiden, a very careful scholar for his time, predicted that no reader of his book would be able to impugn his data or his way of treating them, but his Catholic adversaries, undeterred, soon announced that they had found eleven thousand lies and errors in his history of the Reformation.[27]

To be sure, some historians recognized the danger of revealing their attachments, and they tried to guard against it. Camden, arming himself against "Prejudice and Affection," said that he had "scarcely . . . anywhere" interposed his own opinion in his annals of Elizabeth (whom he idolized, as he admitted).[28] Daniel refused to comment on the facts that he had brought together because he thought he had no right to color his material.[29] Defining the function of so-called civil history as the linking of events to causes, Bacon insisted that the writer be impartial, "not wasting time, after the manner of critics, in praise and blame, but simply narrating the fact historically, with but slight intermixture of private judgment."[30] Raleigh – a chief offender for reading history in the light of his opinions – severely censured Livy for being overpartial to the Romans.[31] Edmund Bolton declared "Indifferency, and even dealing" to be the "Glory" of historians.[32] Milton, despite his own intensely partisan view of Reformation history, judged others by an austere standard, and castigated writers like Boece because they put their own affections over truth and wrote to "magnify their country."[33] Hobbes called Thucydides the best of all historians because he refused to stop the flow of his narration to speculate about the "secret aymes" and "inward cogitations" of the men whose actions he recorded. For this reason the historian of the Peloponnesian War, "though he never digresse to read a Lecture, Morall or Political, upon his owne Text, nor enter into mens hearts, further then the actions themselves evidently guide him, is yet accounted the most Politique Historiographer that ever writ."[34]

Most historians, however, would not recognize the force of these restrictions, for despite their boasted obligation to record the naked truth of things – whatever that might mean – they were at best committed to the partial truths, and even the distortions and evasions, of church or state or party. As a result, their work acquired the function of persuasion and instruction, and on occasion it became the tool of propaganda.

This extended use of history was anything but new. Indeed, it had produced the first great triumph of Christian historiography, and if none of Augustine's successors had equalled his success they at any rate had built a strong tradition of loading history with a heavy freight of politics and morals, to say nothing of theology. As one example out of many, but one well known to the Elizabethans, we may cite the contemporary accounts of Richard II's deposition. Although the chroniclers present the same array of "facts" about this celebrated and portentous episode, their interpretations of these facts are so grotesquely different that they range from adoration to abuse. To

Jean Créton, a Frenchman who had witnessed some of the events that he records, Richard is a great and greatly suffering man whose own misdeeds are minimized, whose afflictions are ascribed to fate and Henry Bolingbroke, and whose melodious complaints are meant to stir our pity and affection. "Thus oftentimes spake King Richard," says Créton about one of his hero's artful lamentations, "sighing piteously from his heart: so that I solemnly protest more than a hundred times I shed many a tear for him. There lives not a man so hard-hearted or so firm, who would not have wept at the sight of the disgrace that was brought upon him."[35] On the other hand, John Gower, Chaucer's moral friend, is so persistently Lancastrian that he treats Henry's usurpation as a providential blessing. Gower announces in the preface to his *Cronica Tripertita* that he will show how God had "cast the hateful Richard from his throne and . . . decided upon the glorious elevation of the pious Henry," and after a relentlessly hostile account of the wicked king's career he writes an epilogue to underscore his meaning: "Let those who are wise beware as they look upon this, for God abominates rulers on earth who live evilly. He who is a sinner cannot be a ruler; as Richard is my witness, his end proves this clearly."[36] Thomas Walsingham, precentor of the great scriptorium of St. Albans and still our chief authority for the period, is not so virulent as Gower, but his hostility to Richard and to the House of York is apparent, as when, for instance, he reports the withering and reviving of the laurels through the realm and the drying-up of the river near Bedford – *aqua profundissima* – as signs of God's displeasure for Woodstock's murder at Calais.[37]

An even more striking example of political dis-
coloration is John Hardyng's account of early fif-
teenth-century history, which was carried on by
Richard Grafton and so led into the stream of Elizabethan chronicles. A retainer of the Percies who had
fought at Agincourt, Hardyng wrote the first version
of his history about the middle of the century with a
strong Lancastrian bias and a dedication to Henry VI.
Apparently disappointed by the king's response, he
promptly undertook a second version for his new
patron, Richard, Duke of York, for whose benefit
he changed the tone to Yorkist; and when Richard
died before the completion of this second draft, about
1465, he addressed it, toward the end, to Edward IV.[38]
One almost regrets that Hardyng died too soon to
celebrate the union of the Red Rose with the White
and to profit from the Tudors.

Characteristically, however, Henry VII did not
leave these things to chance: he imported Polydore
Vergil, an erudite Italian, to rewrite the annals of his
realm in a way not soothing to the few surviving
Yorkists, and thus he launched the string of Tudor
chronicles that served Shakespeare and his fellows
when they turned history into literature. Vergil was
a man of learning and, as we shall see, of a certain
independence, but he clearly comprehended what his
royal master wanted; and for the most part his successors such as Grafton, Hall, and Holinshed – who
cribbed from him and one another – managed to com-
bine commercial enterprise and devotion to the House
of Tudor with tolerable success. One of the authentic
masterpieces of sixteenth-century historiography, and
also of Tudor propaganda, was More's life of Richard
III. First printed by Grafton in his lumbering con-

tinuation of Hardyng's *Chronicle* in 1543 and thereafter used by Hall and by almost all the others, it converted the last Yorkist king of England into a bogeyman for all good subjects of the Tudors; and thanks to Shakespeare, the portrait, or the caricature, survives despite the corrections of later and less prejudiced historians. On the other hand, it would seem that Henry VIII really was a moral monster, but in reading Hall's glowing record of his reign we are willing to forget the fact, and to submerge the lecher and the tyrant in the hero of the English Reformation.

Such extreme partisanship was not without its danger. Hall's book, with its assertive Protestantism, found a ready market in the reign of Edward VI, but it was duly banned and burned by Mary – just as, a generation later, certain sections of the second (1587) edition of Holinshed were canceled and replaced with less offensive matter at the direct order of the Privy Council. George Cavendish's splendid life of Wolsey affords another cautionary example. Apparently written in the reign of Mary, its publication was at the time unthinkable; and although it was known and used in manuscript by Stow, it did not appear in print until 1641, and then in a hideously mangled version that emphasized the danger of ecclesiastics meddling in affairs of state – a thesis clearly aimed at Laud.

Such episodes, which were common through the period, permit a painful inference: that the historian could discharge his obligation to the truth only if the truth did not offend. Although this tacit restriction was most apparent in the treatment of contemporary affairs, it was sometimes felt by those who dealt with history incidentally, and whose subjects were remote. For example, most of the events described in the abortive first (1555) edition of *A Mirror for Magis-trates* were as distant from Queen Mary as Napoleon is from us; none the less its publication was abruptly "hyndred" while the work was going through the press, and it did not appear until a new queen sat upon the throne and its contents were "perused & licenced."[39]

In *Sejanus*, half a century later, Jonson had pro-phetically shown what happens to the historian who, under the pretext of recording past events, "doth taxe the present state,"[40] for it was owing to this very play, as he told William Drummond, that he was haled before the Privy Council on a charge of "popperie and treason."[41] Jonson's comments on the cruelty, injustice, and immorality of rulers could perhaps have been con-fused with treason, but it is hard to see how "pop-perie" could have crept into a play about imperial Rome. About the same time, Daniel, too, was brought before the Privy Council on the charge of having used his newly published play *Philotas* to make seditious comments on the troubles of the Earl of Essex, and although he was eventually exonerated, he recorded his dismay, and his muted indignation, in a pair of painful letters.[42] Whether or not Shakespeare changed Sir John Oldcastle to Falstaff in order to dissociate his fat knight from the Lollard martyr (whose descendants may have been annoyed), in the epilogue to *2 Henry IV* he seems to apologize for the confusion. This, like the deletion, ordered by the Master of the Revels, of the insurrection scene from *The Book of Sir Thomas More*, may not be a clear example of art made tongue-tied by authority, but the queen herself was troubled by the success of Shakespeare's *Richard II*, and it was surely not through editorial caprice that the deposition scene was cut from all the quartos printed in her time.

A more brutal kind of force was exercised against John Hayward, a young lawyer and an amateur historian who unluckily chose to open his career with an elaborate reconstruction of the causes and the circumstances of Richard II's deposition. Prefaced by a fulsome Latin dedication to the Earl of Essex, *The First Part of the Life and Reign of King Henry IV* appeared early in 1599, and at once became a *cause célèbre*. Although Bacon wittily remarked that the author had been guilty of nothing more than felony – for having plagiarized so much from Tacitus – the queen smelled treason in the book, and her reaction was intense. First, the offensive dedication was abruptly ordered canceled; then, a few months later, the second edition, although sterilized by an "Epistle Apologeticall," was gathered up and burned; and finally, in July, after Essex had embarked upon his disastrous Irish expedition, Hayward was subjected to severe interrogation. These proceedings, which Sir Edward Coke conducted and for which his notes survive, made things look very black. In resurrecting a story two hundred years old, said Coke, Hayward had intended "the application of it to this tyme," for he showed a weak and ineffectual ruler, a corrupt and selfish council, a group of discontented nobles, and a commons "groning" under harsh taxation. And hereupon, Coke concluded grimly, "the king is deposed." Denying any seditious intention, Hayward tried to justify his book, but following a second interrogation in 1601 he was committed to the Tower, and there, it seems, he stayed until the old queen died.[43] Meanwhile it was ordered by the Privy Council that no more works on English history should appear without express approval.[44] Years later, when

Hayward's fortunes had revived, he told Prince Henry that writing history was a dangerous line of work, for even if an author deals with "men long since dead, and whose posteritie is cleane worne out," he runs a fearful risk.[45]

Few historians needed Hayward's hard instruction to know the truth of this assertion. Back in the days of Edward VI, when Thomas Cooper undertook to continue Lanquet's uncompleted chronicle and to bring it up to date, he was at first exhilarated by the prospect of dealing with an age so "weightie" and diverse. What a chance for writing history, he exclaimed: to show

how continuall warres have bene betwene two the most mightie prynces of Europe the Emperour and the Frenche kynge? how many debates betwene England France and Scotlande? how great alteracion of religion? how many rebellions? how divers warres? how great persecucions for the same in Germanie, Englande, Denmarke, Boheme, Spaigne, France and Italy? what change of prynces? what alteracion of common lawes? how many enormities newly spronge up among the people of all countreis?

But prudence, or perhaps the printer, got the better of his valor, and he settled for the statement of a few bare facts because he feared that any "odyous judgement" of his own would surely give offense.[46]

The greatest of Elizabethan annalists understood these matters very well. Even though Camden used the queen's own "Rolls, Memorials and Records" in writing of her reign[47] – for after all he undertook the work at Burleigh's instigation and therefore had a very special status – he was careful not to press his luck too far. "Things manifest and evident I have not concealed," he said; "Things doubtfull I have interpreted favourably; Things secret and abstruse I have not pried into."[48] He mentions, for example, that after the defeat of the Armada it was feared that James, already "exasperated" by his mother's recent execution, would throw his weight to Spain. To prevent this, and "to pacifie his Mind," the queen's ambassador offered him an English dukedom, a very handsome pension, a household guard, and other bits of bounty; but whether this was done on the ambassador's own initiative "or by Command of others," Camden says laconically, he neither knew nor did he try to ascertain.[49] His precept, like his practice, would seem to illustrate the rule of thumb that the anonymous author of a poem on Mary Queen of Scots devised: unless a ruler brings destruction on his realm, this prudent writer said, one should hide his "secret vices," deal gently with his "Doubtfull faultes," and be patient with his wrongs.[50]

For obvious reasons, most historians had no knowledge of what Camden called "Things secret and abstruse." Richard Knolles, for instance, was denied the use of all official records while working on his *General History of the Turks*,[51] and even Fulke Greville, with his superb connections, was also unsuccessful when he asked Sir Robert Cecil if he could examine the "Records of the Councell-chest" for a projected history of the late queen's reign. When Cecil, after some equivocation and delay, inquired more closely into his intentions, Greville explained that although he thought a historian should tell nothing but the truth, he should also exercise discretion, for

to tell all truths were both justly to wrong, and offend not only Princes, and States, but to blemish, and stir up against himselfe, the frailty and tendernesse, not only of particular men, but of many Families, with the spirit of an Athenian Timon.

His doubt still unresolved, however, Cecil turned him down because, as he finally explained, the council-chests could not be used without the king's own "approbation."[52]

Such approbation would be very slow in coming from King James, for despite his own pretensions as a man of learning he did not care for independent scholars. Like his predecessor, who discouraged research in ancient documents because she feared that new-found facts and unremembered precedents might disturb the status quo,[53] he was quick to take offense at any sign of disrespect, and to make his disapproval known. Conversely, he gloried in the sort of adulation that one contemporary historian supplied when he announced that James's "Chastitie, Patience, Pietie, Mercie, and Judgement, Wisedome, Learning, Bountie, Peace, and Munificence" were themes of universal adulation.[54] Daniel was therefore being merely prudent when he said that he would not "usurpe" upon the "liberty" that this great king had given scholars, but "tread as tenderly on the graves of his magnificent Progenitors, as possibly I can: Knowing there may (in a kind) be *Laesa Maiestas*, even against dead Princes."[55] Although the British Solomon recommended to his son such "authentick" histories as the *Commentaries* of Caesar, he thought that anyone who even owned the "in-famous invectives" of Buchanan and Knox should be punished for their crime.[56] In 1614, when a group of distinguished scholars undertook to revive the Society of Antiquaries, which had been established in the 1580's and then allowed to lapse, they agreed that "for avoiding Offence" there should be no meddling with religion or affairs of state; none the less, as Sir Henry Spelman later told the story, before the second meeting of the group

we had notice that his Majesty took a little Mislike of our Society; not being inform'd, that we were resolv'd to decline all Matters of State. Yet hereupon we forbare to meet again, and so all our Labours lost.[57]

It was in this same year that the most exemplary work of Christian providential history in the English Renaissance incurred the king's displeasure. Raleigh, who knew the cost of royal disapproval, declared that "whosoever, in writing a modern history, shall follow truth too near the heels, it may happily strike out his teeth."[58] He had therefore thought, no doubt, that since his own work came no closer to the present than the Roman conquest of Greece in 130 B.C. it could hardly give offense, but no sooner had *The History of the World* appeared than it was "called in by the Kinges commaundment" and scrutinized for various indiscretions, "specially for beeing too sawcie in censuring princes." Although the ban was only temporary, it was a bitter blow to Raleigh, according to the gossip of the day, "for he thought he had won his spurres and pleased the King extraordinarilie."[59] He should have known, of course, that James, despite the flattery which he himself received,[60] would pounce upon that passage in the preface which illustrates the theme of retribution with a catalogue of royal crimes.[61]

And so the record runs. Three years after Raleigh's execution, Peter Heylin – of all people – almost blasted his career before it started by comparing France and England in a way displeasing to the king. In 1627 Sir

Robert Cotton, the great collector who had assisted with his learning and his books such men as Camden, Speed, and Bacon, encountered royal opposition for his work on Henry III, which was viewed in certain quarters as an attack upon King Charles. As a scholar who used his erudition in support of Parliamentary power, Cotton posed a certain threat to Charles, of course, but what about Sir Francis Hubert? When, in 1628, this very minor poet learned to his dismay that a poem on Edward II, which he had written in his salad days some thirty years before, had been exhumed and printed, he hastened to disclaim a work "so nakedly, so unworthily, so mangled and so maymed thrust into the world,"[62] and he promptly undertook an authorized edition that deleted anything offensive to the conscience of the king. Such episodes, some grave and some absurd, not only indicate a problem that anyone who dealt with history had to face; they also indicate a drastic limitation on the high ideal of truth.

▢ Another limitation was that which we may call the theological. It was customary, of course, to distinguish various kinds of history. Jean Bodin classified them as human, natural, and divine (which he described respectively as probable, inevitable, and holy);[63] Bacon classified them as natural, civil, ecclesiastical, and literary;[64] Degory Wheare as divine, natural, political, and ecclesiastical.[65] Whatever the refinements of these and other schemes, however, they did not prevent confusion, which reveals itself in two conspicuous but contradictory ways: as timidity about assessing so-called sacred history by the tests applied to other kinds of knowledge, and as boldness in referring to the will of God events whose causes are unknown. Despite a widespread tonic discontent with old-fashioned chroniclers whose inelegance and imprecision rendered them absurd, virtually all Renaissance historians drew upon the Bible, but almost none of them dared treat the data drawn from Scripture with the candor they deserved. Not only, therefore, could the uncritical acceptance of material thought to be divinely sanctioned stifle fresh investigation, but the facile logic by which providence, as an expression of the will of God, was identified with local, patriotic ends or with the writer's own convictions could turn history into propaganda or into moral exhortation. Needless to say, both of these procedures tended to obscure the shining image of the truth.

Historians, with their almost statutory devotion to the truth (for "theyr lippes sound of things doone, and veritie be written in theyr fore-heads"),[66] were bound to look upon the Bible as supreme. As a record of events that occurred in place and time it had to be regarded as absolutely and uniquely true; as a demonstration of God's direction over His creation it exemplified, *par excellence*, a utility for moral and instructive ends; as the product of what Raleigh called "those happy hands which the Holy Ghost hath guided"[67] it superseded other works of history and also acted as a check upon their errors and distortions. It is therefore not surprising that undergraduates at Oxford were told, as late as 1623, that

it is the Sacred History onely which discovers the secrets of the most remote Antiquity, and never lies: It is the Sacred History alone, which gives a faithful testimony of the Succession of times from the very beginning of all things, and never makes one false step. She alone is the most shining light of the Eternal Truth.

And to conclude, she alone is the best Mistress of Life, and absolutely perfect.[68]

As we may infer from such encomiastic comments, which are scattered thick throughout the period, the superiority of sacred to profane history was a topic never staled by repetition. The first of the unique distinctions of sacred history was, of course, its absolute veracity. Speaking for the scholar, Edmund Bolton invoked the Bible – "whose majesty no Attick, nor Tullian Eloquence can express, nor to whose Entireness of Verity any human Wit, or Diligence can come near" – as the prototype of style and truth;[69] and speaking for the general public, Richard Brathwaite, who never strayed beyond the commonplace, said that it was "drained from the pure Spring of Cœlestiall Wisedome, and therefore impossible to erre either in Action or Relation."[70] It was for this reason, an Elizabethan chronologer explained, that his work would settle all disputes about the date and sequence of events, for whereas the Grecian, Roman, Persian, and gentile historians had "missed the square and perfect frame of the Prophets, the streight and perfect line from Adam unto Christ," he himself had made "the Sacred Histories the Centre and grounde of all beginnings, and the onely proofe of all antiquities, without which (sayeth Eusebius) no Historie can be true."[71] On the same principle, Milton, at the beginning of his *History of Britain*, declared that only those nations of whom the "sacred books have spoken" could be certain of their origins, for all the others were unknown.[72] In addition to its truth, sacred history was alleged to be supreme because, as one sixteenth-century writer said, it gave "testimonies" of those "workes of God" that were unperceived and therefore unrecorded by the "gentiles."[73] It was, then, a precedent of unimpeachable authority for those, like Augustine and his successors, who viewed the course of all events as the slow unfolding of a providential purpose. When Raleigh said that sacred history was better than profane, which is cluttered up with second causes, because the former shows God's plan for His creation, he gave one expression to this major theme;[74] and Milton gave another when he declared that "historical faith" – defined as "an assent to the truth of scripture history, and to sound doctrine" – was essential to salvation.[75]

It is Raleigh, of course, who best exemplifies the strength and weakness of this Christian view of history in the later Renaissance. Whereas almost everyone subscribed, at least in theory, to the notions just rehearsed, he put them into use, for as the author of *The History of the World* he accepted what the Bible said as unerring and unquestioned truth, and he relied on data drawn from reason and research only when the Scriptures failed.[76] It was for this reason that Arnold, in his famous inaugural lecture "On the Modern Element in Literature," called Raleigh obsolete, and ridiculed his interminable discussions about the nature of the firmament and the geography of Eden;[77] but *The History of the World* was a product of its age, and its success was overwhelming.

Like Bacon, but in a different way and for a different reason, Raleigh drew a sharp distinction between revealed and natural knowledge, between the certain truth bestowed by God and recorded in the Bible and the doubtful findings of our own investigations. As a consequence, he treats one kind of data like a priest, and the other like a skeptic. Sacred history, he asserted, has a "singular prerogative" over anything produced by "merely human authors" because "it setteth down expressly the true and first causes of all that happened";[78] on the other hand, profane history is mainly a matter of conjecture, where we look for second causes and try to reconstruct, as best we can with our impaired resources and imperfect information, a scrappy record and a faulty explanation of events. One produces knowledge, the other guesswork and opinion; for, whatever men's secret or unacknowledged motives, God's design is clear and steady, and we may read it in His sacred word. Just as He afflicted Rehoboam, son of Solomon, for instance, so he has dealt with all transgressors, and the Bible tells us why:

> The same just God, who liveth and governeth all things for ever, doth in these our times give victory, courage, and discourage, raise and throw down kings, estates, cities, and nations, for the same offences which were committed of old, and are committed in the present: for which reason, in these and other the afflictions of Israel, always the causes are set down, that they might be as precedents to succeeding ages.[79]

Raleigh has, in fact, a double standard. He gives the same belief to sacred history, as he says in quoting Augustine, that one would give the Gospel if one had seen it written by the very hand of God,[80] but he handles other kinds of data with verve and play and erudition. For example, having shown that the conflicting accounts of Fabius the Roman and Philinus the Carthaginian about the Battle of Cannae are riddled with error and deceit, he points out that in a case like this a writer must rely upon his own resources "observe the coherence of things; and believe so much only to be true, as dependeth upon good reason, or (at least) fair probability."[81] Conversely, he concludes a survey of clashing, erudite opinions about the location of Mount Ararat by appealing to "that judge which cannot err, even to the world of truth,"[82] and he resolves a problem of Old Testament genealogy, made muddy by research, with this disarming explanation:

I have thought it not superfluous here in this place to shew by what means it was possible that some error might have crept into the history of those times, and thereby have brought us to a needless trouble of searching out the truth, as it were by candle-light, in the uncertain fragments of lost authors, which we might have found by daylight, had we adhered only to the scriptures.[83]

When there is, or seems to be, a conflict between the sacred and profane accounts of this or that event — for instance, between Isaiah, Jeremiah, and Ezekiel as opposed to Herodotus and Diodorus about Nebuchadnezzar's invasion of Egypt — he always follows Scripture;[84] and even when he deals with things not mentioned in the Bible he often reads into events a Christian providential meaning by exercising what he calls a freedom of conjecture[85] — that is, by the attribution of a moral purpose to events for which he thinks a merely natural explanation insufficient. Thus Cyrus the Great is depicted as "an instrument of God's power, used for the chastising of many nations, and the establishing of a government in those parts of the world, which was not long to continue";[86] the Athenian disaster at Syracuse is cited as a proof that when God intends to punish people He makes their rulers mad;[87] and Alexander is presented as one sent "to erect and cast down again, to establish and to destroy, and to bring all things, persons and states to the same certain ends, which the infinite Spirit of the Universal, piercing, moving, and governing all things, hath ordained."[88]

If this glib recourse to divine causality accounted for much of Raleigh's contemporary success it has not enhanced his later reputation. Like Sir Thomas Browne,[89] he thought that merely natural explanations left everything important unexplained, and he was always on the watch for moral purpose. The cheese-wife knows as well as the philosopher, he said, "that sour runnet doth coagulate her milk into a curd," but when we ask "whereby" and "how" this comes about, we are forced to seek a higher cause than that advanced by Aristotle and his latter-day disciples;[90] and so at last we come to God, to whom the great events of history, no less than sour milk, must be assigned.

There is not therefore the smallest accident which may seem unto men as falling out by chance, and of no consequence, but that the same is caused by God to effect somewhat else by; yea, and oftentimes to effect things of the greatest worldly importance, either presently or in many years after, when the occasions are either not considered or forgotten.[91]

By this commodious principle, all history, profane as well as sacred, asserts the same divine intentions. Even when these intentions are expressed through natural operations or by means of second causes – as when Pharaoh's cruelty moved his daughter to protect the little Moses who would one day lead and save the chosen people[92] – they impart the same conviction as when God shows His hand directly, and they lead us to the highest knowledge, which is a humble recognition of His power.[93]

As all the rivers in the world, though they have divers risings and divers runnings, though they sometimes hide themselves for a while under ground, and seem to be lost in sea-like lakes, do at last find, and fall into the great ocean; so, after all the searches that human capacity hath, and after all philosophical contemplation and curiosity, in the necessity of this infinite power, all the reason of man ends and dissolves itself.[94]

We shall return to Raleigh later, but we have said enough, perhaps, to suggest that his juxtaposed and contradictory attitudes toward truth, together with his bent for reading history as the demonstration of divine control, establish his credential as a Renaissance historian.

# the Use
# of history

If, as we have seen, one main prop of history as a form of writing was, or was supposed to be, its truth, another was its value as instruction. When John Stow, perhaps the ablest and most indefatigable of Elizabethan chroniclers, came to assess his work of almost forty years he was proudest of its pedagogic function. It was as hard for a reader of history to be "without some colours of wisedome, invitements to vertue, and loathing of naughty facts," he said in retrospect, "as it is for a well favoured man to walke up and downe in the hote parching sunne, and not to be therewith sun-burned."[1] Although not all historians would accept the homely figure, none would challenge the assertion, for instruction was the "end and scope" of history, as Sir Walter Raleigh said,[2] and no historian mindful of his duty could neglect his proper function. History could give pleasure too, of course, through the charm and strength of its narration, but when the first Camden professor of the subject at Oxford remarked compendiously that "History is nothing but Moral Philosophy, cloathed in Examples,"[3] he merely summarized the orthodox opinion. The truth and therefore use of history were, in fact, so tirelessly reiterated that they acquired a formulaic sanction.

One ample, famous statement of this commonplace was Jacques Amyot's preface to his great translation of Plutarch, which, in Sir Thomas North's still greater version, was read by Shakespeare and apparently by everybody else in England. Defining history as "an orderly register of notable things sayd, done, or happened in tyme past, to mainteyne the continuall remembraunce of them, and to serve for the instruction of them to come,"[4] Amyot undertook to prove "Historiographers" better than philosophers because they do not merely state but by their skill exemplify a proper course of action, and better than poets because, scorning to "inrich things by commending them above the starrs and their deserving," they repose upon the truth.[5] Therefore, as Sir Thomas North himself declared, their works "are fit for every place, reache to all persons, serve for all tymes, teache the living, revive the dead."[6] It was on these very grounds, of course, that Sidney's historian thought himself supreme. Whereas the moral philosopher – whom, significantly, he regarded as a major rival – talks about a merely "disputative vertue," he shows how virtue was exemplified at Marathon and Agincourt, for he gives life to precept by example. If the "fine-witted" philosopher makes the songbook, he explains, "I put the learners handle to the Lute: and if he be the guide, I am the light."[7]

Under the broad rubric of instruction the benefits of history were so variously described, depending on the writer's own concern with politics or morals or theology, that they could be adapted to almost any special purpose. For example, Thomas Cooper, a future bishop of the Church of England, viewed history as a register of those rewarded for obeying God and those chastized for insubordination,[8] whereas Thomas Beard, a Puritan schoolmaster one of whose pupils was Oliver

Cromwell, viewed it as a terrifying proof that God was "armed with thunder, fire, and a bloody sword" to annihilate all sinners – by far the greater portion of mankind.[9] Those of a less muscular piety, on the other hand, liked to think of history as a set of cautionary examples to protect us from the dangers of experience. "What can be thought more pleasaunt or profitable," asked one influential humanist, "then sytting as it were in the Theatre or Stage of mans life (the whiche an Historye hath most exquisitely furnished in all points . . .) to be made ware and wyse at the perilles of other men, without any daunger on his owne behalfe?"[10] Sir Thomas North concurred, but he used doggerel to put the matter more succinctly:

> A happie wight is he that by mishappes
> Of others, doth beware of afterclappes.[11]

History as a school of moral action was a standard and prolific theme. As the dying Hamlet thought, and as Sir John Hayward said,[12] it is history that preserves the good man's glory and the bad man's shame, and permits them to survive their own extinction in the record of their deeds. Thus it was that Fulke Greville wrote his famous life of Sidney not merely as a tribute to a noble friend but as a "Sea-mark" for his countrymen, who, guided by the memory of his fame, might "learn to sayl through the straits of true vertue, into a calm, and spacious Ocean of human honour."[13] Arthur Golding, who, despite his famous Ovid, mainly worked on sterner stuff like Calvin's commentaries and Protestant propaganda, construed all history, sacred and profane, as moving toward a single goal: "thadvancement of Vertue, and the defacying of Vyce."[14] John Foxe, the martyrologist, was somewhat more exclusive but no less pedagogic. The historian's only proper subject, he maintained, was "the lives, acts, and doings, not of bloody warriors, but of the mild and constant martyrs of Christ," and his only proper business was "to encourage men to all kind of christian godliness."[15] Though less intent on doing good than Foxe, even the fastidious George Puttenham, whose main concern was belletristic expertise, assumed a moral stance when, in *The Art of English Poesy*, he came to talk of history. It is pre-eminently the kind of writing, he explained, that teaches man "sound judgment and perfect worldly wisedome," and that leaves him with "a stedfast resolution" to control his own behavior.[16]

The same instructive commonplaces turned up even in escapist literature when hucksters like William Painter and Geoffrey Fenton cited them to justify their versions of *novelle* and romances. "In these histories (which by an other terme I call Novells)," said Painter of the frisky tales in *The Palace of Pleasure*, "both old and yonge may lerne how to avoyde y$^e$ ruine, overthrow, inconvenience, and displeasure, that lascivious desire and wanton wil doth bring to their suters and pursuers";[17] and Fenton, unctuously citing Cicero, also identified his lush, erotic work as history and insisted on its moral purpose.[18] When Sir Walter Raleigh, battered by the force of circumstance and Jacobean politics, said that history taught us resignation "by the comparison and application of other men's fore-passed miseries with our own like errors and ill deservings,"[19] he was no doubt thinking of a rather different moral purpose, but like North and Fenton and the others he reworked the basic theme of history as instruction.

A more specific aspect of this theme was history as

a school of politics. Despite his evil reputation with Elizabethans, Machiavelli provides a good example here, for whatever the English thought, or professed to think, about him as a moralist, they could hardly take exception to his utilitarian view of history as instruction. He himself explained that he composed his *Discourses* not to venerate an ancient shrine but to derive certain general principles of political behavior from facts that Livy had observed, and to show how they could be applied in modern times;[20] and it was for the same reason that he undertook to tell the story of his native city, which he thought his predecessors had bungled in recording. "If any lesson be useful to citizens who govern republics," he said, "it is a knowledge of the causes of animosities and divisions in commonwealths; by which they may be made wise by the fate of others, and learn to preserve their union."[21] Disregarding moralistic platitudes, he read history to learn the source and exercise of power, and therefore some of his conclusions were bound to be repugnant. To try to prove from Livy, for example, that most successful politicians rise by fraud instead of force, and that compulsory promises need not be observed,[22] struck Sir Thomas Browne as wicked: it is "the rhetoric of Satan," he protested, which could "pervert a loose or prejudicate belief."[23] As Bacon recognized, however, the *Discourses* were the "fittest" kind of writing for instruction in the craft of politics, for being built on fact instead of preconceived opinion, they made the study of the past a guide to present action, and therefore they exemplified a major benefit of history.[24] It is ironical that Machiavelli's conclusions gave such deep offense, for his method was employed, or at any rate endorsed, by every orthodox historian.

To represent the orthodox historian we may summon Richard Stanyhurst, one of Holinshed's contributors whose bad eminence in English literature rests on his translation of the *Aeneid* in quantitative verse. His history of Ireland is a scrappy piece of work, but as he described its merits to Sir Philip Sidney's father, the lord-deputy of that unhappy island, he made it sound supremely useful to a man in his position. Here you will find, said Stanyhurst, "vice punished, vertue rewarded, rebellion suppressed, loyaltie exalted, haughtinesse disliked, courtesie beloved, briberie detested, justice imbraced, polling officers to their perpetuall shame reprooved, and upright governours to their eternal fame extolled."[25] Camden would have smiled at this perhaps, but his own more modest comment on the work that he had done is built upon the same assumptions. "I shall esteem myself fully recompensed for my Labour," he remarked, "if by my ready Willingnesse to preserve the Memory of Things, to relate the Truth, and to train up the Minds of men to Honesty and Wisedom, I may thereby find a Place amongst the petty Writers of great Matters."[26] In a similar vein John Selden said that he had conducted his researches not "to shew barely what hath been . . . but to give other light to the Practice & doubts of the present."[27] Like Thomas Wilson, who described the earliest English translation of Demosthenes as a book "most nedeful to be redde" by those who prize "their Countries libertie and desire to take warning for their better avayle, by example of others,"[28] or like Sir John Davies, who exhaustively explored the mistakes of English rule in Ireland to provide a key for new and better policies,[29] Selden thought that a "too studious Affectation of bare and sterile Antiquitie . . . [is]

nothing els but to be exceeding busy about nothing," whereas a fruitful study of the past could illuminate the present and prepare us for the future.[30]

It was therefore often pointed out that "Princes, yea and all other, that have auctoritee in great affaires and high matters"[31] should apply themselves to history for instruction in the use of power, and conversely that historians themselves, as Bodin and Bacon said, should not be "closet penmen" but persons with a first-hand knowledge of politics and war.[32] History, as Montaigne observed, is "a nursery of ethical and political dissertations, for the benefit and improvement of those who hold a place in the management of the world."[33] *A Mirror for Magistrates*, that perennial best-seller of the later sixteenth century, was expressly put together, as its compiler said, for "the nobilitye and all other in office" as a manual of political behavior. "Here as in a loking glas," he told the magnates of the realm, "you shall see (if any vice be in you) howe the like hath bene punished in other heretofore, whereby admonished, I trust it will be a good occasion to move you to the soner amendment. This is the chiefest ende, whye it is set furth, which God graunt it may attayne."[34] Thomas Wilson[35] and Thomas Blundeville[36] used the same argument couched more circumspectly, in dedicating their historical works to Cecil and the Earl of Leicester respectively, and a generation later James VI of Scotland – perhaps a better scholar than king – suggested to his heir the study of "authentick" histories as a preparation for the burden and the glory of the crown.[37] He was no doubt pleased, therefore, when Bacon urged Prince Charles to acquaint himself with Henry VII's triumphs and reversals so that he might be instructed by example,[38] and it was with the same

Charles's "approbation" and "encouragement" that Edward Hyde, in 1646, undertook to write "a full and clear narration of the grounds, circumstances, and artifices" of the rebellion that had brought a mighty king so low.[39]

☐ Another favorite theme, but one with much more literary and philosophical significance, was history as a refuge from devouring time. That youth and strength and beauty fade, that summer yields to autumn, that mighty states decline and fall are facts that all men everywhere have known, but in the Renaissance these facts were felt, and many times recorded, with extraordinary precision. When we are shown Old Age, in Thomas Sackville's great "Induction," peering with his hollow eyes upon the earth to which he must so soon return[40] we feel the Elizabethan shudder at the thought of time and its unflagging work of demolition; and when Spenser, in perhaps the last lines that he wrote, dreams of that great "Sabbaoth" when time and change shall have a stop and come to rest "upon the pillours of eternity" he gives consummate statement to a Renaissance ideal.[41] Although mutability can hardly be regarded as a Renaissance invention, it clearly held a special fascination for Shakespeare and his fellows. It appears in countless lyric poems on the downward course of love and beauty to the cold obstruction of the grave; in a vast array of sermons, Puritan and other, about the vanity of life and the terror of its close; in the charnel-house perversities of Cyril Tourneur and many other Jacobeans; in Taylor's mortuary prose; in the somber splendors of Sir Thomas Browne.

We should keep in mind, however, that all these

graves and worms and epitaphs were emblems, of a sort, for time; that time meant alteration; and that alteration meant attrition and decay. If the limp versifying on these topics in Spenser's early poems or the lumbering dismay of *A Mirror for Magistrates* now seems merely quaint, there are dozens of authentic masterworks that show us how the problems of devouring time could stir great writers when they were writing at their best. One thinks of the final scene in *Doctor Faustus;* of an older Spenser's two great cantos, with their pomp and steady power; of Romeo and Juliet as they snatch at fleeting joy while rushing toward the grave; of Daniel's deep-toned meditation as he wonders which of man's endeavors might be won upon the mighty waste of days; of Donne's acute but morbid speculations on mortality; of the dust that closes Helen's eye in Nashe's lovely, terrifying song; of young Lycidas, dead ere his prime; of Herrick's fragile but enduring charm when he sings of Time's trans-shifting; of Marvell's invitation to his coy mistress, with its witty and controlled despair. But most of all, of course, one thinks of Shakespeare's sonnets, where time is treated with a polyphonic grandeur unmatched in English literature.

Despite its range and beauty, this complex literary response was contained within a system that made, or seemed to make, the facts of time and change intelligible, for in the Christian view of history, time could be reduced to limits, and change could be ascribed to God's own purpose and control. When the Fathers of the Church declared that just as God had brought the whole creation into being, so He would bring it to a close, they made a revolution in historiography. They converted history from a string of endless cycles or a random sequence of events whose cause and purpose are unknown into a linear process with a beginning and an end – a process planned by God, marked by certain episodes of incalculable significance, and moving toward a goal that would fulfil divine intentions. This Christian view of history, which received its first great literary expression in Augustine's *City of God* and which retained its main configurations through the Renaissance, did not, of course, obliterate the facts of time and change, but it did provide a set of explanations. It gave time dimensions, and change a moral purpose that men could comprehend, for it enabled them to look on time and change, and on the world itself, as finite, co-extensive segments of a great design to be completed in eternity[42] – that "one permanent point, without succession, parts, flux or division"[43] from which all history flows and to which it must, at God's command, return. As Hooker says with characteristic grandeur, "God's own eternity is the hand which leadeth Angels in the course of their perpetuity; their perpetuity is the hand that draweth out celestial motion, the line of which motion and the thread of time are spun together."[44]

In the Christian scheme of history, then, time is viewed against eternity, and the two are brought into alignment. When Augustine cried out to God that "Thy To-day, is Eternity"[45] he reduced to epigram and paradox the double theme of God's transcendence to the realm of time and change and also His control of it, and by this paradox he dominated man's approach to history for a thousand years or more. We talk about the past, the present, and the future, Donne observed in imitation of a famous passage in Augustine's *Confessions*,[46] but since one has ceased to be and the other is to come, we are chained to a recurrent moment that disintegrates and reconstructs itself;[47] and just as we are captured in the ceaseless flow of time until God releases us into eternity, so time itself is set to run its course until, with one decisive stroke, God brings it to a predetermined close. Even the most resolute opponents of the widely shared conviction that time was near its end conceded that the end would surely come, and that, as one of them explained, "the whole world with all the parts and workes thereof . . . shall bee totally and finally dissolved and annihilated: As they were made out of nothing, so into nothing shall they return againe."[48] If, then, time provides the matrix in which a timeless purpose is attained, time and change themselves acquire dimensions in eternity, and history – no longer just a record of events – becomes a statement of divine intentions as they are manifested in creation. This, of course, is Michael's view of history as he predicts "the race of time" for Adam at the end of *Paradise Lost*, and Adam's gratitude and acquiescence[49] may be regarded as the orthodox response to so divine a plan.

This plan had obvious implications for men who wrote and studied history. Although most of them, like Sir Thomas Browne, could not speak of eternity without a solecism or think thereof without an ecstasy,[50] anyone could comprehend the tidy span of several thousand years or so that stretched from the creation to the birth of Christ and thence unto the final conflagration. The first of these events was dated variously – by Luther in 4000 B.C., by Scaliger in 3949, by Raleigh in 4032, by Bishop Ussher in 4004 – and although the final act of this great drama, which depended solely on the secret will of God, could not be dated with precision, its coming was assured. When the dying Hotspur said that time, which "takes survey of all the world, Must have a stop,"[51] he was thinking of his own demise; but when Donne, with apocalyptic rapture, foretold the dawning of that final day toward which all history moved as toward its consummation, he was thinking of the death of time itself. "I shall rise from the grave," he said,

and never misse this City, which shall be no where, for I shall see the City of God, the new Jerusalem. I shall looke up, and never wonder when it will be day, for, the Angell will tell me that time shall be no more, and I shall see, and see cheerefully that last day, the day of judgement, which shall have no night, never end, and be united to the Antient of dayes, to God himselfe, who had no morning, never began.[52]

Not only were time and history framed by narrow limits, but the events comprising them were clustered into more or less co-equal periods that traced a linear progression. In Augustine's arrangement, for example, the major epochs – most of them precisely fourteen generations long – run from Adam to the flood, from the flood to Abraham, from Abraham to David, and so on to the Incarnation – that pivotal event that ushered in the present age, which itself would end with the destruction of the world and be followed by eternity.[53] The rage for viewing history as a string of epochs, each defined and dated by something so stupendous as the creation, the fall, the flood, or the nativity, was so strong throughout the Middle Ages that Roger of Wendover and Matthew Paris, the great Benedictine annalists of the early thirteenth century, built their works upon this plan, and it persisted through the Renaissance by the force of sheer inertia. Thus it was that chroniclers like Thomas Cooper and John Stow could rework the ancient schemes;[54] that Raleigh was enchanted by chronology; that Peter Heylin, with crushing finality, could announce the age of the world as 5,576 years – "neither more nor less."[55] One common variation of Augustine's chronology was that proposed by Vives in the early sixteenth century and paraphrased by Donne in 1626, when he compared the relentless march of time to the stillness of eternity:

In all the two thousand yeares of Nature, before the Law given by Moses, And the two thousand yeares of Law, before the Gospel given by Christ; and the two thousand yeares of Grace, which are running now, (of which last houre we have heard three quarters strike, more then fifteen hundred of this last two thousand spent) In all this six thousand, in all those, which God may be pleased to adde, *In domo patris*, In this House of his Fathers, there was never heard quarter clock to strike, never seen minute glasse to turne.[56]

Although such periodic schemes were particularly appropriate for treating sacred history, they had other uses too. When John Foxe sketched his *Acts and Monuments* he planned to write five books, each of which would trace three hundred years of persecution. At first it seemed to be a simple plan: three centuries from Christ to Constantine's conversion, three more for the expansion of the Church, three more for the "declining" time of true religion, and so on; but when he came to treat the last three hundred years, Foxe found that he required eight new books to write about the Reformation, and so the scheme collapsed.[57] Undeterred by this example, Edmund Howes (who continued John Stow's *Annales*) tried to squeeze all English history into six coequal periods, each punctuated by a major "Alteration." Thus the first epoch, the reign of Trojan Brut and his descendants from 1000 to 500 B.C., ended with the death of Gorboduc, the second with the conquest of the Romans, the third with the coming of the Saxons, the fourth with the Danish and Norman invasions ("a double blow as it were in the necke one of another within a few yeares"), the fifth with the Henrician reformation, and the sixth with the Messianic reign of James I.[58]

Such periodic and apocalyptic schemes were particularly attractive to those who viewed the world as rushing to destruction. The rise and fall of the so-called Four Monarchies of Babylon, Persia, Greece, and Rome that the prophet Daniel saw[59] was a favorite theme with Protestant historians because it enabled them to link the dissolution of the Roman Empire with the advent of the Reformation, and thus to view the present age – "so full fraught with affliction and calamitie as never was before, or ever shall be hereafter" – as the prelude to the end of time.[60] It was for this reason that the great Johannes Sleiden could construe the history of the early sixteenth century as the ending of a universal drama, which he recorded with "astonishment" and "Wonder."[61] Similarly, but a century later and for a somewhat different reason, a prominent Anglican historian could invoke the prophecy of the Four Monarchies to predict the speedy dissolution of the world unless the English changed their wicked ways and turned Cromwell out of office.[62] Even men who took a calmer view of politics were certain, as Sir Walter Raleigh said, that the "long day of mankind" was sinking into night and that "the world's tragedy and time" were in their final stage.[63] For example, Owen Felltham was not certain that the end would come in 1656 – a date commonly predicted because its distance from the incarnation matched the span from Adam to the flood – but he knew, by "the most infallible pre-monitors of a dissolution," that it was not far off;[64] and Sir Thomas Browne was so convinced that "the great mutations of the world are acted" that he thought "time may be too short" for living men's designs.[65] The most imposing, or at any rate the most relentless, statement of this apocalyptic theme was Godfrey Goodman's *Fall of Man*, a massive demonstration that all of human history, owing to the sin of Adam, records the process of decay, and that the process was accelerating as the world approached its own extinction. In terms of bulk alone, to say nothing of of its unremitting gloom, Bishop Goodman's work – which was published in the year of Shakespeare's death – marks perhaps the most extreme invasion of history by theology.

The idea of cyclic alteration, another variation of the theme of providential history, may be regarded as both alternative and antidote to the gloom of these apocalyptic schemes. It was, of course, a very ancient notion. "One generation passeth away, and another generation cometh," the nameless author of Ecclesiastes said,

but the earth abideth for ever. The sun also ariseth, and the sun goeth down, and hasteth to his place where he arose. The wind goeth toward the south, and turneth about unto the north; it whirleth about continually, and the wind returneth again according to his circuits.[66]

This theme of periodic change, which rested on the seasonal, biological, and political facts of every man's experience, was, of course, a commonplace in pagan literature. Cyclic repetitions of strength and weakness, prosperity and adversity, were basic to the Hellenic view of history; Plato, in the *Statesman*, made a myth about the rhythmic alteration of good and evil in the world;[67] and the Stoics built their metaphysics on the doctrine of recurrence.

For reasons noted earlier, however, the Fathers of the Church could not accept what Augustine had called "the unreal and futile cycles of the godless."[68] They viewed history not as a process of endless repetitions without direction, purpose, or control, but as the finite, ordered movement of events, each of them appointed to a certain stage in time and each of them unique. Christ died only once, said Augustine, and he would never die again.[69] Everything that happened earlier was by way of preparation; everything that followed was a consequence; and the movement of the whole was toward a consummation that would justify the course and history and mark the end of time.

Although this linear, periodic, and providential view of history would seem to be incompatible with the notion of cyclic alteration, both could be accommodated within the Christian scheme of things, and both found ardent advocates in the later Renaissance. Everyone agreed, of course, that the universe would end in flames, but since the limits of the present, final epoch were known to God alone, men could only speculate about the date of judgment day. Those who thought it near at hand announced the wrath to come and indulged their apocalyptic schemes, whereas those who envisioned endless tracts of time before the final conflagration foretold, with some serenity, a continuation of the status quo. Within the status quo, moreover, they construed the rhythmic pulse of time and change as proof of cyclic alteration, and cyclic alteration as proof of God's control.

The most enthusiastic spokesman for this latter view was George Hakewill, a young Anglican clergyman who wrote his famous *Apology or Declaration of the Power and Providence of God in the Government of the World* as a systematic refutation of Bishop Goodman's melancholy *Fall of Man*. Hakewill contended that the indefinite duration of the world was a necessary hypothesis because it enabled men to recognize in God's creation the attributes of His divinity. Eternity, the first of these attributes, is best imagined as a circle, and therefore the world and all its works are fashioned like a sphere, he said, and exhibit periodic alteration.

So are the celestiall bodies both the orbs and the starres, so are the elements; the motions of the heavens are likewise Circular, the transmutation of the elements circular, the generation and corruption of the mixt bodies circular; the akorne springing from the oake, and the oake againe from the akorne; the egge from the henne, and the henne againe from the egge; the rivers running into the sea, and returning from the sea againe; Corruption treading upon the heels of generation, & generation againe upon the heels of corruption; the spring upon the heels of winter, summer of the spring, autumne of the summer, winter of autumne, and the spring upon winter againe. . . . And thus the whole world by dauncing the rounds is perpetuated, & by this perpetuation represents the eternity of the maker thereof.[70]

Hakewill holds, in other words, that although time and change afflict all things, the shifting surface of events exhibits cyclic alteration, and therefore the basic rhythm of recurrence is a kind of hieroglyph for the preservation of the universe itself.[71]

Like Spenser's *Two Cantos of Mutability*, Hakewill's work may be regarded as the learned, subtle demonstration of a commonplace, for despite the problems of adjusting a cyclic to a linear view of change, the notion of pattern and recurrence, from which derived the major benefit of history as a series of examples, was essential to the Renaissance historian. Machiavelli did not, of course, refer such things to God, but when he explained, in speaking of the rise and fall of institutions, that "Virtue is the mother of peace; peace produces idleness; idleness begets disorder, and disorder brings ruin," he thought that he had found the natural sequence of events.[72] So did Richard Knolles, in his *General History of the Turks*, when he ascribed a similar set of changes to "the inevitable course of destinie, or more truely to say, unto the fatal doome of the most highest."[73] Jean Bodin, who elaborately refuted the Four Monarchies of the prophet Daniel as a "long-established, but mistaken" notion,[74] detected in the rise and fall of cultures a periodic alteration that invalidated all apocalyptic schemes. "Since these things are so," he said, "and since by some eternall law of nature the path of change seems to go in a circle, so that vices press upon virtues, ignorance upon knowledge, base upon honorable, and darkness upon light, they are mistaken who think that the race of men always deteriorates."[75]

Cyclic alteration, though put in somewhat darker terms, is also one of Samuel Daniel's standard themes. When, in *Musophilus*, he invokes those

> blessed Letters, that combine in one
> All ages past, and makes one live with all,

it is to celebrate the "Knowledge" which instructs and civilizes men through example and design;[76] and when,

in the dedication to *Philotas,* he cites the "represent-
ments of times past" it is to show recurrence as a key
to human action.[77] In *Cleopatra* the theme is even more
explicit. There the philosopher Arius refers the sad
estate of things in Egypt to "An ancient Canon, of
eternall date" by which all kingdoms rise and fall.

> Thus doth the ever-changing course of things
> Runne a perpetuall circle, ever turning:
> And that same day that hiest glory brings,
> Brings us unto the point of backe-returning.[78]

This metaphor of history as a wheel or circle occurs a
thousand times in Elizabethan literature, and it retains
its charm for writers well into the age of Hobbes and
Milton. When Milton himself employs it in the conclusion to his *History of Britain* he reiterates a standard
theme of Renaissance historiography;[79] and when
Browne, with characteristic wit and splendor, talks
about the "revolution and vicissitude" of men and
states and even of the universe itself, he converts an
ancient commonplace to art.[80]

Somewhat less artful was its use by sixteenth-
century chroniclers. Although committed to the propo-
sition that the advent of the Tudors was a blessing
preordained by God, they were none the less obliged
to register the crimes, follies, and misfortunes that, as
Gibbon tells us, constitute the history of mankind;
and sometimes, as we read their heavy, shapeless
books, we think that crime and folly and misfortune
were all they wrote about. But if their subject was
disorder and misrule, their works exemplify, and often
explicate, the notion that history is not a string of
inconsequential episodes but an intelligible design,
where repetition and recurrence provide the key to
explanation. The world depicted here was not without

its perils; it was plagued by bold, bad men, and it seemed to reel from one disaster to another; but beneath the surface perturbation there was – or so the Tudors liked to think – a rhythm that announced itself in periodic change, and a morally significant sequence of crime and retribution that served the purpose of example and instruction. Thus Edward Hall was moved to treat the troubles of the fifteenth century, he explains, "so that all men (more clerer then the sonne) maie apparantly perceive, that as by discord greate thynges decaie and fall to ruine, so the same by concord be revived and erected";[81] and when Daniel, working through the same material, cites "the deformities of Civile Dissension, and the miserable events of Rebellions, Conspiracies, and bloudy Revengements, which followed (as in a circle) upon that breach in the due course of Succession by the Usurpation of Hen. 4," he completes the circle by referring to the "happinesse of an established Government" that the Tudors had secured.[82] This is also Holinshed's procedure, and, broadly speaking, it is Shakespeare's in the first tetralogy, where mounting political and moral disorder is presented, however crudely, as expiation for the primal fault of Richard II's deposition and as prologue for the triumph of the Tudors.

These and cognate notions rest upon the widely shared conviction that history is not the record of a random sequence of events but the record of a process, linear or cyclic or maybe even both, that defines the moral contour of events. This conviction, in turn, rests upon the idea of providence, the broadest and the most persistently employed principle of causality in Renaissance historiography. It may be crudely summarized as follows: everything that happens – from the fall of a sparrow through the vicissitudes of private men and the calamities of rulers to the wheeling of the stars in their majestic courses – exemplifies God's providential care of His creation; for just as He made the universe, so He sustains its operations, and He directs the course of history in accordance with a purpose that, though often hidden, is bound to be benign.

In a system that identified causality with moral purpose there was, of course, no room for chance or fickle fortune. Generations of theologians, moralists, and historians who could agree on little else agreed that what appears as chance or aberration would, if fully understood, reveal a causal sequence expressive of divine intention. What foolish men call fortune, Sir Thomas Browne explained, is in fact "that serpentine and crooked line" whereby God "draws those actions that his wisdom intends in a more unknown and secret way."

Abraham might have thought the ram in the thicket came thither by accident; human reason would have said that mere chance conveyed Moses in the ark to the sight of Pharaoh's daughter. What a labyrinth is there in the story of Joseph, able to convert a Stoic! Surely there are in every man's life certain rubs, doublings and wrenches which pass awhile under the effects of chance, but at the last, well examined, prove the mere hand of God.

And Browne goes on, inevitably, to cite the discovery of the Gunpowder Plot and the defeat of the Armada as effects whose causes could only be regarded as divine.[83]

As Calvin pointed out, those who hold the vague philosophical belief that "somehow the world is under divine government, and yet imagine the workings of

providence in a confused way, as though God paid no
attention to individual creatures" are guilty of an error
that Christ himself exposed, for to ascribe events to
fortune is to impugn the sovereignty of God.[84] In one
form or another this theme turns up everywhere in
literature: in *A Mirror for Magistrates*, where the
notion of retributive justice as an instrument of divine
providence replaces fortune's whirling wheel; in the
maze of Spenser's Faeryland, to which the clew is
providential intervention; even in the rant of Tambur-
laine, whose assertion that

> I hold the Fates bound fast in iron chains,
> And with my hand turn Fortune's wheel about

was contrived to make the groundlings murmur in
dismay.[85] The historian, we learn from the preface to
Plutarch's *Lives*, serves only as a "register to set
downe the judgements and definitive sentences of
Gods Court," some of which are clear to natural reason
and some of which must baffle understanding, but if
he assigns to fortune things he cannot fully comprehend, he shows that he is "dazeled" by the brightness
and "confounded" by the depth of God's transcendent
power.[86] Milton would of course concur, for when
young he wrote about "that power Which erring men
call chance,"[87] and when old he wrote about a God who
said that "what I will is fate."[88] Although Bacon tried
to prove that fortune is nothing but a superstitious
term for second causes, whose operations we can trace
and comprehend,[89] Raleigh spoke for most of his contemporaries when he called fate the obedience of second causes to the first, and showed that even nature
was alive with moral purpose.[90]

In large terms, therefore, to hold that apparent evil works toward good, that even fallen nature, though sunk in sin and temporality, is part of God's design, that death leads into life and time into eternity, is to find direction in the movement of events. On a smaller scale, to hold that history does repeat itself is to find recurrent causal sequences and archetypal situations, particularly in politics and government, by which we guide our own behavior. Because these were notions broad enough and vague enough to serve the most conflicting interests, they were cited in a thousand different ways, some of them as easy and as vulgar as cartoons, some of them sublime. In general, of course, the theme is most imposing when stated in its largest terms. When Hooker, for example, defines providence as a universal striving toward a final good as determined "in the purity of God's own knowledge and will" it is to show that time and change and history are instrumental to a grand design;[91] and Milton's effort to assert eternal providence and justify the ways of God to man has such grandeur of conception that even sin and death, the marks of man's indignity, become the means of his redemption.

To descend from these conceptual splendors to a somewhat lower plane of providential explanation we may see that the ancient habit of reading history as theology might serve at least to unify and organize one's approach to one's material. John Foxe, for instance, could view fifteen hundred years of European history as "the wonderful operation of Christ's mighty hand, ever working in his church";[92] so urbane a man as Sir Henry Wotton could think that King John, Edward II, Richard II, Henry VI, and Richard III had been expressly sent by God to emphasize, by way of contrast, "the Wisdom, Goodness, Prudence, and Lenity of their Predecessors";[93] and a Puritan like Edward Johnson, the author of *The Wonder-Working Providence of Sion's Saviour*, could explain the settlement of New England as a feat ordained by God to dismay the "multitude of irreligious lascivious and popish affected persons" who had overspread the realm of Charles I.[94]

But when we descend yet lower, to the vulgarities and absurdities of specific providential explanations for particular events, we can see at once why so many historians of the later Renaissance were eager to reform their own procedures. Not all chroniclers were so indefatigable and inspirational as Thomas Beard, who, "to the end that the drousie consciences of Gods children might be awakened, and the desperat hearts of the wicked be confounded," ransacked his predecessors' work for cautionary anecdotes about tyrants, apostates, heretics, hypocrites, necromancers, epicures and atheists (one of whom was Marlowe), idolators, perjurers, blasphemers, anti-sabbatarians, "rebellious and stubborn children," political malcontents, murderers, adulterers, rapists, perverts, drunkards, robbers, tax collectors, and usurers; but many were as quick as Beard to look for moral meanings in events.[95] For example, George Hakewill explained the new star of 1572 as a "supernaturall and miraculous worke of Almighty God" to commemorate the massacre of St. Bartholomew's Day;[96] Robert Burton attributed Columbus' discovery of America if not to God's own skill in navigation at least to His direction of the voyage;[97] Sir Edward Peyton explained the plague at Charles I's accession as a judgment on the new king's reign, "God pointing to us, as with a fescu, as a school-master, to warn us to repent of our abominable sins; if no admonition would reform us, he would scourge us with an iron rod."[98] Such instances could be multiplied indefinitely, but a single episode from one of Abraham Fleming's additions to the second edition of Holinshed's *Chronicles* – the book that Shakespeare knew so well – will serve to show the depths of providential history. Writing as a virulent anti-Catholic, and drawing much from Foxe, Fleming tells of Bishop Stephen Gardiner's waiting impatiently for the news of Ridley's and Latimer's execution. When, finally, the messenger arrived from Oxford with the glad tidings that the heretics were dead, Gardiner called at once for dinner.

Now, saith he, let us go to dinner. Whereupon, they being set downe, meat was immediately brought, and the bishop began merilie to eate: but what followed? The bloudie tyrant had not eaten a few bits, but the sudden stroke of God his terrible hand fell upon him in such sort, as immediatlie he was taken from the table, and so brought to his bed, where he continued the space of fifteene daies, in such intollerable anguish and torments, that all that meane while, during those fifteene daies, he could not avoid by order of urine, or otherwise, any thing that he received: whereby his bodie being miserablie inflamed within (who had inflamed so manie good martyrs before) was brought to a wretched end. And thereof no doubt, as most like is, came the thrusting out of his toong from his mouth so swolne and blacke, with the inflamation of his bodie. A spectacle worthie to be noted and beholden of all such bloudie burning persecutors.[99]

Although Edmund Bolton, a contemporary of Selden, Speed, and Bacon, and himself a relatively advanced student of historiography, said that it was the first duty of historians "to discover God's Assistances,

Disappointments and Overruling in human affairs; . . .
to establish the just Fear of his celestial Majesty against
Atheists, and Voluptuaries, for the general good of
Mankind, and the World,"[100] even he would disap-
prove of Fleming's facile, vulgar moralizing.

# the Form
# of history

Earlier in this series we attempted to survey some of those assumptions felt as facts, as Mr. Whitehead used to say, to which most Renaissance historians subscribed. It now remains to go behind the well-rubbed slogans in order to determine their relation to the style and form of history, to note some transformations in the historian's own conception of his methods and procedure, and to indicate, perhaps, the slow beginnings of reform.

If disaffection is essential to reform it would seem that most historians in the later Renaissance were ripe for change and innovation, for they almost unanimously viewed their precessors' work with a mixture of disdain and condescension. Whatever posterity may think – if it thinks at all – about the achievement of such historians as Edmund Bolton and Degory Wheare, they and most of their contemporaries thought it marked a real advance. Men who could read Tacitus and Livy, to say nothing of Thucydides, were not likely to be stirred by Hardyng or to emulate the work of Grafton, and for a variety of reasons – social, religious, and political – they argued that a new and better kind of history was required.

As early as the middle of the sixteenth century William Baldwin, the editor of *A Mirror for Magistrates*, had complained about "Unfruytfull Fabyan" and Edward Hall, one of whom was so intent on facts and dates that he "let the causes slip" and the other so timid and equivocating that he confused his reader with conflicting explanations.

> But seing causes are the chiefest thinges
> That should be noted of the story wryters,
> That men may learne what endes al causes bringes
> They be unwurthy the name of Croniclers,
> That leave them cleane out of their registers.
> Or doubtfully report them: for the fruite
> Of reading stories, standeth in the suite.[1]

About the same time that Baldwin uttered these un-metrical complaints, Roger Ascham, who regarded Caesar and Livy as the best of all historians, sneered at Hall's "Indenture English"[2] and implied that only Thomas More, in his famous piece on Richard III, had not disgraced his native tongue.[3] A generation later Thomas Nashe expressed a lofty condescension toward what he called the "lay Chronigraphers, that write of nothing but of Mayors and Sheriefs, and the deare yeare, and the great Frost," because they lacked the style and knowledge to deal with greater things.[4] Im-pelled by very different motives, John Foxe said that he began his *Acts and Monuments* to correct the errors and distortions of the "multitude of chronicle and history-writers," most of whom were either monks or "clients to the See of Rome," and therefore thoroughly unreliable.[5] Bacon, who otherwise did not have much in common with the martyrologist, also disapproved of monkish historians on the ground that they were ill equipped to deal with politics, a subject that only those "acquainted with the difficulties and mysteries of state business" were qualified to treat.[6] Of the writers who had tried to cope with the "dignity and difficulty" of civil history, the former attorney-general and lord chancellor observed, some wrote "only barren and commonplace narratives, a very reproach to history"; some jumbled facts together; some lost themselves, and their readers, in "minutest particularities"; some indulged themselves in "bold inventions"; some, "ever thinking of their party," wrote only out of passion; some were doctrinaire; some composed "orations and harangues"; and in short, "among all the writings of men, there is nothing rarer than a true and perfect Civil History."[7]

Not all historians of Bacon's generation were so sweeping in their disapproval, but most of them were discontented. For example, Daniel said that he wrote his *History of England* for purely patriotic reasons, there being no people since the Romans who had "fought so many battailes prosperously" or who had been so badly served by their historians. "And therefore out of tender remorse, to see these men defrauded of their glory so deerely bought, and their affaires confusedly delivered, I was drawne (though the least able for such a worke) to make this adventure."[8] King James's eldest son, a precocious and discriminating patron of the arts, was concerned about this problem too. "Shall our actions, shall our conditions be described by every bungling hand," he asked. "Shall every filthie finger defile our reputation? Shall our Honour be basely buried in the drosse of rude and absurd writings?" Sir John Hayward, who reports this conversation, was ready with a set of explanations: that most men of education and experience were too much employed in public matters to undertake research, that they were fearful lest they give offense, and that "the Argument of our English histories hath been so foiled heretofore by some unworthie writers, that men of qualitie may esteeme themselves discredited by dealing in it."[9]

This reminds one of the fastidious Edmund Bolton, who thought that "among the greatest wants in our ancient Authors, are the wants of Art and Style,"[10] and who deplored what he called those "vast vulgar Tomes procured for the most part by the husbandry of Printers" (by which he no doubt meant the works of Grafton, Holinshed, and Stow).[11] They were "warehouses," he complained, "where stuffe lyes in fardles, and heapes unwrought, packt up together by unskilfull chroniclers," whereas the kind of history needed was that which presents "choise things" by expounding "premisses, executions, and sequels, the causes, counsels, occasions, and most vitall circumstances of the worthy matter which they deliver."[12]

Although John Speed – who, like Stow, was trained to be a tailor – carried on the Tudor tradition of massive, annalistic history, he shared some of Bolton's reservations and also some of his ideals. When he remarks of Polydore Vergil, for example, that this patriarch of Tudor chroniclers assigned "causes to actions, not alwayes such as are, but such as seemed to him most probable, not seldome confounding and changing persons, times, names, and things,"[13] he reflects the interests and the standards of a newer generation – a generation that Camden had instructed and that Selden was adorning.

But in this and other things there were no sudden innovations. Although John Stow, who was born when Thomas More was still alive, cited some three hundred fifty sources (manuscript and other) for the last edition of his *Annals*, Selden complained that except for Camden's annals of Elizabeth and Bacon's life of Henry VII not a single "publique piece" of English history was built upon enough research. As befitted such a polymath, he believed in primary sources, for he thought that to attempt a solid piece of work without the "carefull searching" of the records of the Exchequer, the Court of Chancery, the Parliamentary archives, and the various episcopal collections was "to spend that time & cost in plastering onely, or painting of a weake and poore building, which should be imployed in provision of timber and stone for the strengthening and inlarging it."[14] Although one can hardly question this ideal, it is odd that Selden looked to Bacon for example, for whereas Camden's scholarship was overwhelming, Bacon's was defective. To be sure, he called truth the sovereign good of human nature and wrote largely of the duties of historians, but he knew or cared so little about research that he thought "any tolerable chronicle" could supply the data that a man of taste required for the more important work of explanation and analysis.[15] Although he wrote the life of Henry VII under difficult conditions, he drew heavily and uncritically upon those sixteenth-century chroniclers whom he himself had deprecated; and he was so careless of his facts that he confused the sequence of events and even missed the date of Henry VII's death. On the other hand, Daniel, who did not display his erudition, merely named the standard printed sources for his *History of England*, but "so that the Reader shall be sure to be payd with no counterfeit Coyne"[16] he took care to document his manuscript materials and even planned to print their texts in an appendix. Unfortunately, this plan was not fulfilled, but a generation later Lord Herbert's massive *Life and Reign of King Henry the Eighth* (1649) offered ample demonstration that a bygone age could be recovered through the labors of research.

As we might expect, Milton's attitude toward earlier English historians is compounded of his deep commitment to reformed religion and his humanistic erudition. Although his commonplace book swarms with references to a staggering list of sources – among others, Bede, William of Malmesbury, Holinshed, Foxe, Stow, Speed, Camden, Buchanan, Edmund Campion, Hayward, and Raleigh, to say nothing of the classics and the Continental writers[17] – he found little to admire in those who dealt with England. "If the Athenians, as some say, made their small deeds great and renowned by their eloquent writers," he remarked with some asperity, "England hath had her noble achievements made small by the unskilful handling of monks, and mechanics."[18] It was "our homebred monks," of course, whom he found most offensive, in part because their politics were vile,[19] in part because of their religion.[20] Bede was bad enough, he said, but even worse were his successors, whose "obscure and blockish chronicles" it was a "labour" to peruse and a "penance" to recall.[21] It is ironical that a man who ranked Sallust first among historians[22] should have been obliged to base his major work of history on "illiterate and frivolous" chroniclers whom he held in great contempt.[23] His attitude is best revealed, perhaps, in that section of the *History of Britain* where he passes from the Roman to the Saxon period, for with the fall of Roman power, he said, there

fell also what before in this Western world was chiefly Roman;

learning, valour, eloquence, history, civility, and even language itself, all these together, as it were, with equal peace, diminishing and decaying. Henceforth we are to steer [in the Middle Ages] by another sort of authors; near enough to the things they write, as in their own country, if that would serve; in time not much belated, some of equal age; in expression barbarous, and to say how judicious, I suspend awhile: this we must expect; in civil matters to find them dubious relaters, and still to the best advantage of what they term the Holy Church, meaning indeed themselves: in most other matters of religion, blind, astonished, and struck with superstition as with a planet; in one word, Monks.[24]

To bring these disrespectful comments to a close we may cite the mighty Clarendon. Although his opinion of his predecessors – including some of those just mentioned – was almost as low as Milton's, he talked less about their monkish superstition than about their inexperience in politics and war. A man of great affairs himself, he thought that only those who had a part in making history (like Polybius, Livy, and Tacitus) were qualified to write it. Whereas such eminent Continental historians as Enrico Caterino Davila and Cardinal Bentivoglio were magnates who could "instruct the ablest and wisest men how to write, and terrify them from writing," he said, their English counterparts were mainly monks and scribblers who "had no other excuse for their presumption but their good-will." Since they themselves lacked learning, skill, and worldly wisdom, their work, inevitably, was clumsy and jejune.[25]

☐ It is significant that although these writers, representing various shades of bigotry and snobbery and real discrimination, have much to say about the historian's methods of research and preparation, his arrangement of materials, and his investigation of the causes and the consequences of events, they reveal no great concern with style. Far from sharing the fascination with stylistic problems that characterizes the poets of the age, they hardly speak of them at all, and when they do it is to voice their disaffection or indifference rather than prescribe reform.

The fact is that style and form were topics that belonged to literature, and despite the vogue, in the later sixteenth century, of poems and plays based on ostensibly historical subjects, the traditional distinction between literature and history was maintained and even strengthened. To be sure, Daniel – perhaps with *The Faerie Queene* in mind – demanded more "veritie" in poems that dealt with English history, "Whence new immortall Iliads might proceed."[26] Spenser acknowledged the objections to his "famous antique history" as merely "painted forgery,"[27] but he none the less persisted in the fiction. Drayton's revision of such early poems as *Piers Gaveston*, *Matilda*, and *Robert, Duke of Normandy* led to a reduction of the erotic and the merely ornamental, and conversely to an accelerated tempo of narration. However, none of these poets advocated turning poetry into history, or even thought the terms convertible.

Such works as *A Mirror for Magistrates* and its many imitations, or Shakespeare's two tetralogies, or Daniel's *Civil Wars*, or Drayton's *Poly-Olbion* did not obliterate the old distinction; if anything, they sharpened it. They showed that the poet or imaginative writer not only could accommodate material which more and more historians were coming to reject, but could use it with a freedom, and twist it to a function, that those who cared for truth abhorred. Early in the reign of Queen Elizabeth, George Puttenham, while conceding the customary distinction between poetry and history, could argue none the less that historical poetry was the most useful and delightful kind of writing because it blended art with truth, and because its authors could embellish fact with fiction. They "used not the matter so precisely to wish that al they wrote should be accounted true," he said disarmingly,

for that was not needeful nor expedient to the purpose, namely to be used either for example or for pleasure: considering that many times it is seene a fained matter or altogether fabulous, besides that it maketh more mirth than any other, works no lesse good conclusions for example then the most true and veritable, but often times more, because the Poet hath the handling of them to fashion at his pleasure, but not so of th' other [i.e. the historian], which must go according to their veritie, and none otherwise, without the writers great blame.[28]

Although this dictum helps us understand, perhaps, the Elizabethans' fondness for things like *A Mirror for Magistrates* and *Albion's England* and Shakespeare's *Henry IV*, it could hardly serve the purpose of a later generation, which took a somewhat sterner view of truth and disliked to mingle fact with fiction. To represent this later generation we may cite an exasperated critic of the Jacobean period who thought that history plays were foolish. Playgoers who "know the Histories before they see them acted," he said,

are ever ashamed, when they have heard what lyes the Players insert amongst them, and how greatly they deprave them. If they be too long for a Play, they make them curtals; if too short, they enlarge them with many Fables, and whither too long or too short, they corrupt them with a Foole and his Bables.[29]

Such comments reflect the wide conviction, which

even poets shared, that literature and history were not to be confused. The withering of the history play in the reign of James I supplies us one example, but others may be gleaned from literature itself. When Daniel dropped *The Civil Wars* and turned, with some relief, to prose, it was more than just fatigue that led him to the change: it was the hope of doing something else, and of doing it another way. When Milton canvassed subjects for the epic that he planned to write one day he did not exclude a hero drawn from British legend,[30] but in the *History of Britain* he rejected what he called the "grand fable" of Trojan Brut, which he relegated, not without affection and regret, to poetry.[31] By the middle of the seventeenth century a subject that might do for literature could be admitted to a history only with disclaimers.

The distinction between literature and history was as old, almost, as European criticism. To say, as Aristotle said, that poetry is "more philosophical and more serious" than history because it treats what might happen instead of what has happened – that is, it treats an ideal or general truth instead of facts empirically observed – is to say that literature concerns the timeless and the universal, whereas history concerns the temporal and specific.[32] It was on these grounds, no doubt, that Cicero distinguished the requirements of poetry and history as, respectively, pleasure and veracity,[33] and that many critics in the Renaissance held that these two kinds of writing dealt with different things, dealt with them in different ways, and addressed themselves to different ends.

It was, of course, a widely shared assumption that any form of writing was mimetic: that it reproduced or imitated something else, and therefore that its benefit and pleasure derived partly from the subject and partly from the skill and art of presentation. In these terms the more ardent advocates of poetry considered history so inferior that they were reluctant to concede it any belletristic function. Cinthio, for instance, declared that the historian is so much shackled by the base and vulgar things he writes about that he cannot divert or edify his reader.[34] On the assumption that any writer using fact is deprived of full poetic power Castelvetro assigned such historical poets as Lucan and Silius Italicus – or, we may add, Daniel, Drayton, and even Milton – to a lower rank than others.[35] Tasso regarded "feigning" so essential to the higher forms of art that he thought anyone restricted to the truth should be denied the name of poet, and be regarded as a mere historian. "If Lucan is not a poet," he explained, "this is because he is in bondage to the truth of particulars rather than attending to the universal."[36] Men of this persuasion would maintain that the poet, or imaginative writer, not only deals with ideal truth, but that he adorns it with the aid of metrics, metaphor, and fable which the historian does – or should – not use. One creates what Sidney called "another nature" with all the art and style at his command; the other, "tyed not to what should bee but to what is, to the particuler truth of things and not to the general reason of things," records the sober facts that he is not permitted to embellish or transmute.[37]

Ironically, this distinction between the imaginative and liberating truth of literature and the factual and restrictive truth of history could be used by either kind of writer to certify his own procedures and to justify his own pretensions. It occupied a central place, of course, in Sidney's great defense of poetry, but

Spenser drew upon it too in explaining his technique,[38] and so did Fulke Greville when, with reference to his friend's *Arcadia*, he called the "representing of vertues, vices, humours, counsells and actions of men in feigned, and unscandalous Images" the most beneficial kind of writing.[39] It was even used obliquely by the authors of such fantasties as *Selimus* and *Henry VIII*, which, because they were supposed to qualify as history plays, were presented as the cold and edifying truth.

> No fained toy nor forged Tragedie,
> Gentles we here present unto your view,
> But a most lamentable historie
> Which this last age acknowledgeth for true.[40]

Explaining that he wrote his *Sophonisba* as a poet – and with an obvious thrust at Jonson and at the heavy load of learning in the margins of *Sejanus* – Marston said that "to transcribe authors, quote authorities, and translate Latin prose orations into English blank verse, hath, in this subject, been the least aim of my studies."[41] Dekker was careful to inform the readers of his *Whore of Babylon* – a muddy and disordered allegory aimed against the Catholics – that he had not been bound by facts and dates, that he wrote "as a Poet, not as an Historian, and that these two doe not live under one law."[42] Even in Thomas May's *Victorious Reign of King Edward the Third*, an ostensibly historical poem of the 1630's, the author did not touch upon the reverses and calamities of his subject's later years because, as he explained, such events were more appropriate for "an acute Hystorian in Prose, than straines of height for an Heroike Poem."[43]

Conversely, most Renaissance historians who labored this distinction turned it to their own advantage. For one thing, it enabled them, as we have seen, to vaunt themselves upon their deep concern with truth – not the distant, ideal truth that poets talked about, but the useful and authenticated truth whereby a man could be instructed in the moral and political realities that life itself reveals. For another, it emancipated them from art, or at any rate it permitted them to banish style and form as alien to their function. "I have made up my mind," Jean Bodin declared, "that it is practically an impossibility for the man who writes to give pleasure, to impart the truth of the matter also."[44] It is Bacon, of course, who provides the *locus classicus* of this distinction as it appeared to the historian. In a famous passage of *The Advancement of Learning* he explains that since poetry is a product of imagination, it must be regarded as a kind of stylized deceit which falsifies and simplifies experience, and thus satisfies the mind of man with fiction. It is, in short, "feigned history," and its seductions are apparent.

Because the acts or events of true history have not that magnitude which satisfieth the mind of man, poesy feigneth acts and events greater and more heroical; because true history propoundeth the successes and issues of actions not so agreeable to the merits of virtue and vice, therefore poesy feigns them more just in retribution, and more according to revealed providence; because true history representeth actions and events more ordinary and less interchanged, therefore poesy endueth them with more rareness, and more unexpected and alternative variations. So as it appeareth that poesy serveth and conferreth to magnanimity, morality, and to delectation. And therefore it was ever thought to have some participation of divineness, because it doth raise and erect the mind, by submitting the shews of things to the desires of the mind; whereas reason doth buckle and bow the mind unto the nature of things.[45]

These ideas, though rarely put so well, had been the staple of historians for a hundred years or more. In the early sixteenth century, Simon Grynaeus, the author of a widely influential treatise, sternly warned of reading history for amusement, as one might play upon a harp or lute "to drive away the time," for history was, as he believed, instructive, and it therefore had no place for style or charm or pleasing fiction. Just as "Cookes have oftentymes more regard to the belly, then to their maysters commoditie and profite," he remarked in irritation, "even so I would God that the wryters of Hystories, for the most part, sought not so muche to please and entice the Reader."[46]

This admonition was no doubt prompted by the work of such Italian humanists as Bruni, Poggio Bracciolini, and Pontano, those accomplished men of letters who regarded history as a form of literature susceptible to rhetorical and stylistic refinement, and who, by precept and example, urged contemporary historians to correct their own barbarities by systematic imitation of the classics, and particularly of Livy. It would be idle to deny, of course, that Renaissance historians were uninstructed by the humanists – for instance, in a new concern with character, in a preference for the national and even local (as opposed to universal) subjects, in an aversion to the fabulous, in civility and intellectual poise – but most of them resisted elegance, and most of them remained committed to what Ascham called a "playne and open" style.[47]

This commitment was expressed not only by the chroniclers, for whom the parochial and the vernacular were almost bread and butter, but also by the scholars

and translators who professed to venerate the classics.
Except for Sir John Hayward, whose plagiarisms and
literary pretensions prompted one of Bacon's witti-
cisms,[48] most English historians were, if not afraid of
style, at any rate suspicious of its charms as hostile to
instruction. In this regard, as others, Camden helped
to set the norm. This great man, whose erudition was
regarded as a national resource, hardly thought of
style, it seems, but he had very strong opinions on the
use and truth of history. Take away the "Why, How,
and To what end, things have been done," he said in
quoting from Polybius, "and all that remains will
rather be an idle Sport and Foolery, then a profitable
Instruction: and though for the present it may delight,
for the future it cannot profit."[49] Holinshed asserted
that his "speech" was "plaine, without any rhetoricall
shew of eloquence, having rather a regard to simple
truth, than to decking words";[50] and Edmund Howes
justified what he called the "tedious labours of im-
partiall truth" by pointing to his homely, honest prose.
"Expect no fyled phrases," he told the "understanding"
reader, no

Ink-horne termes, uncouth wordes, nor fantastique speeches,
but good playne English without affectation, rightly befitting
Chronologie. If Ciceroes eloquence, Platoes Oratory, or Virgils
loftie verse, be thy chiefe desire: Poules church-yard is now
plentiously furnished to satisfie thee.[51]

Such assertions of rugged simplicity were as routine
for translators as for men like Holinshed and Howes.
Golding, for example, boasted of the bleakness of his
prose, which he described as "voyd of ornate termes
and eloquent indytings," and he expressed the hope
that his translation of Justin in its "playne and homely

English cote" would serve the reader just as well as something "richly clad in Romayn vesture."[52] In his great rendition of Livy, Philemon Holland explained that since his author so pre-eminently exemplified the historian's prime responsibility – "the deliverie of a simple trueth" – he himself had "framed" his pen "not to any affected phrase, but to a meane and popular style."[53] Hobbes was therefore working in an old tradition when he voiced his disapproval of those who made "the scope of History not profit by writing truth, but delight of the hearer, as if it were a Song."[54]

A corollary of these doctrines of simplicity and utility as functions of the truth of history was the aversion to interpolated speeches of the writer's own invention. This device, despite its unimpeachable antiquity and authority, was widely thought to be a form of self-indulgence, an exercise in style and rhetoric, and a distortion of the truth. Daniel used it in *The Civil Wars*, of course, but not even there without apology, and although he cited the precedent of Sallust and Livy he explained that they, in this regard, were writing like the poets.[55] It was as Richard Brathwaite said: "for an Historian . . . to use too polish'd or terse a Style, or to play the Orator, when he should performe the office of a Relator, would not relish of discretion."[56] Johannes Sleiden was so eager to avoid the "Rhetorical Flourishes" which might, he feared, betray his own emotions that even in reporting speeches he turned everything into the same flat prose. "I only furnish the Style, and use my own words," he explained, "that the tenor of my Language may be equal, and always alike."[57] Even if we uncharitably supposed that a man of Thomas Blundeville's modest talent would frown upon the use of feigned orations because they lay beyond his power,[58] we could hardly use this explanation for the most accomplished rhetorician of his age. "The offices of a rhetorician and an historian are as different as the arts which they profess," Milton told a correspondent who had asked for his opinion;[59] and although he said that he liked Sallust best of all the Romans and regarded Tacitus as a "most energetic and animated writer," he refused to take them as his models. One should try to write with "energy and distinctness, with purity and perspicuity of diction," he said. "The decorations of style I do not greatly heed; for I require an historian, and not a rhetorician."[60]

That a man of Milton's gigantic literary resources should, in the posture of historian, express such conventional hostility to the imaginative, the belletristic, and the ornamental may be said to mark the final cleavage between the "feigning" art of literature and the factual truth of history. Within two generations, Sidney, in behalf of art, had emphatically defined the mutually exclusive functions of the poet and historian; and Bacon, for a very different reason, had strengthened the distinction. By the time that Milton wrote the gap had grown so wide and deep that not even he could bridge it. Not in terms of style alone, but in the selection of a subject, in the evaluation and arrangement of materials, and in the shaping of a work according to its predetermined purpose, the author of *Comus* and of the *History of Britain* would appear to be a double man.

☐ Although it would take a shelf of books to trace these topics in detail, to glance in closing at a single facet of the problem will serve, perhaps, to illustrate the main contention: that as the gap between literature

and history deepened, there was less and less exchange
of their methods and materials.

Whatever moved Geoffrey of Monmouth to as-
semble and embellish some charming tales from Welsh
folklore as a history of the British kings, the pleasing
fraud did not go undetected. Although a string of
historians, beginning with Walter of Newburgh and
notably including Polydore Vergil, expressed their
doubt or disbelief, Geoffrey's account of a line of
ancient British heroes that began with Trojan Brut
and came down, through Arthur, to Cadwallader
clearly had a great appeal for poets. It also had a great
appeal for aspiring Tudor politicians, for by com-
bining, as it did, the prophecies of Merlin, the magi-
cian, and Cadwallader, the last Celtic king of Britain
(who was vanquished by the Saxons), it predicted that
the glory of the nation would revive when another
native king regained the throne. It was not entirely
accidental, therefore, that the crafty Welshman Henry
VII named his first-born son Prince Arthur, or that
Geoffrey's captivating fable, with subsequent variations and additions, was embraced as British history.

To be sure, there were skeptics and dissenters.
Pointing to the fact that Geoffrey's tale of Trojan Brut
not only lacked corroboration but was inherently im-
plausible, Polydore Vergil called it an "impudent"
invention compounded of folklore and Celtic moon-
shine.[61] John Rastell, a lawyer whose sister married
Thomas More, was just as bluntly disapproving. "This
story semeth more mervaylous than trewe," he said;
"& though it hath contynued here in englande & taken
for treuth amonge us englysshemen yet other people
do therfore laugh us to scorne & so me semeth they
may right well & I mervayle in my mynde y$^t$ men

having any good naturall reason wyll to such a thinge gyve credence."[62]

But Tudor patriotism, to say nothing of the literary imagination, was not to be deterred by common sense. Outraged by the Italian Polydore's affront to British honor, John Leland undertook the defense of Arthur's historicity, as he explained, "to make tryall of my wit in a matter honest, to helpe the history languishing, to advance the glory of my country, hindred by envy, and beeing enthralled unto the crafty deceiptes of evill willers, restore the same honestly unto liberty."[63] Despite the syntax of this bold assertion – which I quote from the Elizabethan translation of Leland's Latin – the intention was beyond reproach, as most good Tudors thought. Although Leland made a great parade of learning to support a feeble cause, it is clear that he was writing mainly from emotion. His use of ostensibly historical apparatus and procedures to expound the legendary and fabulous juxtaposes literature and history in a way extremely characteristic of the Tudors. Between Leland's heavy Latin prose, almost void of literary appeal, and Spenser's "haughty enterprise" in relating the "chronicle of Briton kings" in the second book of *The Faerie Queene* there would seem to be a thin connection, but the antiquarian and the poet were describing, each in his own way, an imaginative truth that transcended merely formal limitations. It was with the same accommodating ambiguity that Puttenham could write a poem about "the adventures & valiaunces" of King Arthur and his knights, of Bevis of Southampton, and of Guy of Warwick, and describe it as a "little brief Romance or historicall ditty,"[64] and that Drayton could relieve the tedium of his endless *Poly-Olbion* with accounts of

Trojan Brut and his descendants – accounts that Selden, in his learned "Illustrations" of the text, exposed as fables and conjectures.

The so-called British history was used not only by the poets. Leland's work on Arthur was translated, with elaborate commendations, as late as 1582, and a year later Gabriel Harvey's brother Richard published a defense of Brut that enabled Nashe to hail him as a "noble Trojan."[65] In the interests of the truth – "whereunto I levell all my endeavour"[66] – John Stow maintained his faith in Geoffrey's work through many years and many books. In a pot-boiler called *A Brief Chronicle, of the Success of Times, from the Creation of the World, to This Instant* (1611) Anthony Munday scolded modern "Criticks" who would "not beleeve our ancient written Records, although confirmed by Emperors, Kings, Popes, and Parliamentes, neyther the Testimony of Strangers."[67] Edmund Howes went even further, arguing not only for the authenticity but also for the moral value of what he called these "aged Stories." To reject them was imprudent, he asserted, because such edifying judgments on "Idolatry, heresie, crueltie, dissentions, rebellions, murders and confused lusts, registred in our records ought now to be so many Trumpets to summon us to repentance."[68]

Such comments, both assertive and apologetic, reflect a rising opposition to the genial practice of converting fable into history. As early as the middle of the sixteenth century Thomas Cooper expressed the equivocal position that came to be routine for historians of his generation when he said that the legendary history of Britain is

full of errours, and hath in it no manifest apparence of truthe, as being written neither of no auncient tyme, nor yet by no credible historian. For if there had remained any veritable monument of these tymes, surely the worshypful Beda and Gildas, our countreie men, yea and Cesar the conquerour therof, wolde not have omitted them. Never the lesse I will not discent from the common opinion thereof, but will also folowe it as nere as I may.[69]

Holinshed, of course, dared not scrap the British history, but he too was plagued by reservations. "That which seemeth to me most likelie, I have noted," he explained, "beseeching the learned (as I trust they will) in such points of doubtfull antiquities to beare with my skill: sith for ought I know, the matter is not yet decided among the learned, but still they are in controversie about it."[70]

The learned opinion to which Holinshed deferred is best exemplified by Camden's *Britannia* (1586), a book that through successive editions and enlargements, and finally in Philemon Holland's translation (1610), came to be regarded as the very crown and summit of English scholarship. For all his massive erudition, Camden was too respectful of tradition and too mindful of its great appeal and political utility to denounce the British history as a fraud, but from his scrupulous examination and assessment of the evidence only one conclusion could emerge: that whatever happened in the British isles before the landing of the Romans was and no doubt would remain a matter for conjecture.

In this regard, as in others, the *Britannia* was a watershed, for although Geoffrey's fables found a few forlorn or angry advocates in the coming generation, their force was clearly waning. In his *History of England* Daniel refused to trace the legendary kings of Britain because, as he observed, there was no "authenticall warrant" for even their existence, to say nothing of their deeds, and therefore no advantage to be gained by rehearsing their supposed accomplishments.[71] Even Edmund Bolton, who declared himself strongly inclined "to have so much of every Historical Monument, or Historical Tradition maintain'd, as may well be holden without open absurdity," and who would have liked to salvage Geoffrey's work, conceded that its "fables or Discohærencies" – which "no man denyeth" – had made it nugatory.[72] Young John Selden, in his notes on *Poly-Olbion*, was even more emphatic. "It is wished," he said with heavy scorn, either that "the poeticall Monkes" who celebrated Arthur and the rest "had contain themselves within bounds of likelyhood" or that their "exorbitant fictions" had been decently interred together with their other indiscretions.

The sweet grace of an inchanting Poem (as unimitable Pindar affirmes) often compels beliefe; but so farre have the indigested reports of barren and Monkish invention expatiated out of the lists of Truth, that from their intermixed and absurd fauxeties hath proceeded doubt; and, in some, even deniall of what was truth.[73]

As we might expect, Bacon did not indulge himself with doubts; he preferred a blunt denial; and thus he said that the accession of James I should be regarded as proof of the sagacity and statesmanship of Henry VII rather than as "the consummation of superstitious prophecies (the belief of fools, but the talk sometimes of wise men)."[74] By the end of James's reign Polydore Vergil's heresy had become so firmly orthodox that the first Camden professor of history at Oxford declined to speak of Geoffrey's fabrications,[75] and Hakewill used the story of Trojan Brut to illustrate the kind of vulgar error that scholars had exposed but not demolished.[76]

But if the British history lingered on into the age of Hobbes and Locke and Dryden, it was only as a fable, and of use to none but poets. Historians like Sir Richard Baker and Peter Heylin, both writing in the middle of the century, were contemptuous of these legends, but they talked about them none the less. Baker called them "stuff" that might amuse a child, but hardly those of "riper Judgements";[77] and Heylin, in this as in other things extreme, was even sharper in his disapproval. "This is the summe of the Tradition concerning Brute," he said in ending his account, "Which though received in darker times of ignorance, and too much credulity; in these more learned dayes hath been laid aside, as false and fabulous."[78]

It is Milton who should have the final word, however, not because he disagreed with the Bakers and the Heylins of his time, but because he recognized another kind of truth that they knew nothing of. When he tested these old stories against the deep resonance of his literary imagination he thought of them as epic,[79] but in his function as historian he drew a firmer line. Although he acknowledged that what we have "of oldest seeming, hath by the greater part of judicious antiquaries been long rejected for a modern fable,"[80] he refused to think that fable was absurd. On the ground that we are lacking any certain information about the early Britons and that legends may record the memory of an unrecovered primal truth, he rehearsed these fictions once again, and even quoted Spenser,[81] as if to prove their lasting charm. At the end of Book One of his *History of Britain*, when he says farewell to

Geoffrey and then turns to Julius Caesar, it is as if he took his leave of literature and moved into the realm of history.

Thus far, though leaning only on the credit of Geoffrey Monmouth, and his assertors, I yet, for the specified causes, have thought it not beneath my purpose to relate what I found. Whereto I neither oblige the belief of other person, nor overhastily subscribe my own. Nor have I stood with others computing or collating years and chronologies, lest I should be vainly curious about the time and circumstances of things, whereof the substance is so much in doubt. By this time, like one who had set out on his way by night, and travelled through a reigon [*sic*] of smooth or idle dreams, our history now arrives on the confines, where daylight and truth meet us with a clear dawn, representing to our view, though at a far distance, true colours and shapes.[82]

Whatever Milton's own intentions, the ambiguity of this passage may supply us with a valediction to Renaissance historiography, for it reminds us that as the modes of history change, there is loss as well as gain.

# Notes

# 1 The Truth of History

1 James Boswell, *Life of Johnson* (Oxford Standard Authors, 1957), pp. 494-495; cf. p. 628.

2 *An Apologie for Poetrie* in *Elizabethan Critical Essays* (ed. G. Gregory Smith, 2 vols., 1904), I, 162, 164. Hereafter cited as "Smith."

3 Richard Stanyhurst in *Holinshed's Chronicles of England, Scotland, and Ireland* (6 vols., 1807-1808), VI, sig. b4$^r$.

4 John Donne, "Of the Progresse of the Soule," lines 281-298 (*Poems*, ed. H. J. C. Grierson, Oxford Standard Authors, 1933, p. 235).

5 *De Oratore*, II.xv.62.

6 *Institutio Oratoria*, II.iv.2–3.

7 Smith, II, 162.

8 *A Report and Discourse . . . of the affaires and state of Germany* in *English Works* (ed. William Aldis Wright, 1904), p. 126.

9 *Coopers Chronicle . . . newly enlarged and augmented* (1560), sig. a2$^v$.

10 *John Knox's History of the Reformation in Scotland* (ed. William Croft Dickinson, 2 vols., 1950), I, 6.

11 "Thomas N. to the Reader" (no pagination) in Richard Grafton, *A Chronicle at large and meere History of the affayres of Englande and Kinges of the same* (1569).

12 Hugh G. Dick, "Thomas Blundeville's *The true order and Methode of wryting and reading Histories* (1574)," *Huntington Library Quarterly*, no. 2 (January 1940), p. 164. Hereafter cited as "Dick."

13 *Method for the Easy Comprehension of History* (trans. Beatrice Reynolds, 1945), p. 55.

14 *The General History of the Reformation of the Church . . . To*

which is Added, A Continuation To the End of the Council of Trent, in the Year 1562. By Edmund Bohun, Esq. (1689), sig. a2$^r$.

15  *The History of The most Renowned and Victorious Princess Elizabeth, Late Queen of England* (3d ed., 1675), sig. a4$^v$. Hereafter cited as "Camden."

16  *Ibid.,* sig. b4$^r$.

17  "To William Camden," *Epigrammes,* no. 14 (*Ben Jonson,* ed. C. H. Herford and Percy and Evelyn Simpson, VIII, 1947, 31).

18  *The First Part of the Historie of England* (1613), p. 2.

19  *History of the Reign of King Henry VII* in *Works* (ed. James Spedding, Robert Leslie Ellis, and Douglas Denon Heath, 16 vols., 1861-1864), XI, 43.

20  *The Historie of Tithes* (1618), pp. vi, xii–xiii.

21  *Nero Caesar, or Monarchie Depraved. An Hystoricall Worke* (1624), sig. A1$^r$.

22  Sig. A2$^v$.

23  Ed. James Craigie Robertson, 2 vols., 1849, I, xv–xvi.

24  *History of Britain* in *Prose Works* (ed. J. A. St. John, 5 vols., 1848-1853), V, 295-296; cf. V, 228; *Of Reformation in England* in *Prose Works,* II, 380.

25  *History of Britain* in *Prose Works,* V, 185.

26  Peter Heylin, *Cosmographie In Four Bookes. Containing the Chorographie and Historie Of the Whole World, And all the principall Kingdomes, Provinces, Seas, and Isles thereof* (1652), sig. A4$^r$.

27  "An account of the Life of the Learned John Sleiden, and of the Reception of his History" (no pagination), prefixed to *The General History of the Reformation of the Church.*

28  Camden, sig. b2$^r$.

29  *The Collection of the History of England* in *Complete Works in Verse and Prose* (ed. Alexander B. Grosart, 5 vols., 1896), IV, 83.

30  *De Augmentis Scientiarum* in *Works,* VIII, 419-420.

31  *History of the World,* v.i.1 (*Works,* 8 vols., 1829, VI, 3–4).

32  *Hypercritica; or A Rule of Judgment for writing, or reading our History's* in *Ancient Critical Essays upon English Poets and Poësy* (ed. Joseph Haslewood, 2 vols., 1811-1815), p. 231. Hereafter cited as "Bolton."

33  *History of Britain* in *Prose Works,* V, 243.

34  *Eight Bookes of the Peloponesian Warre . . . Interpreted with*

*Faith and Diligence Immediately out of the Greeke By Thomas Hobbes* (1629), sig. A3ʳ–A3ᵛ. Hereafter cited as "Hobbes."

35    "A French Metrical History of the Deposition of King Richard the Second" (trans. John Webb), *Archaelogia*, xx (1824), 116.

36    *Cronica Tripertita* in *Major Latin Works of John Gower* (trans. Eric W. Stockton, 1962), pp. 289, 326.

37    *Historia Anglicana* (ed. Henry Thomas Riley), ii (1864), 229.

38    See Charles L. Kingsford, "The First Version of Hardyng's Chronicle," *English Historical Review*, xxvii (1912), 462-482, 740-753.

39    *The Mirror for Magistrates* (ed. Lily B. Campbell, 1938), p. 66. Hereafter cited as *Mirror*.

40    ii.308 (*Ben Jonson*, ed. Herford and Simpson, iv, 1932, 385).

41    *Ibid.*, i (1925), 141.

42    See *The Tragedy of Philotas* (ed. Laurence Michel, 1949), pp. 36-66; Joan Rees, *Samuel Daniel* (1964), pp. 97-98. For the texts of Daniel's letters (to Cecil and Mountjoy) see *The Tragedy of Philotas*, pp. 37-39.

43    See Margaret Dowling, "Sir John Hayward's Troubles over His *Life of Henry IV*," *Library*, Fourth Series, xi (1930), 212-224. For Bacon's remark on Hayward's plagiarism see *Apothegms*, no. lviii (*Works*, vii, 133).

44    Edward Arber, *Transcript of the Registers of the Company of Stationers of London*, iii (1876), 677.

45    *The Lives of the III. Normans, Kings of England* (1613), sig. A2ʳ–A2ᵛ.

46    *Coopers Chronicle*, sig. a3ʳ–a3ᵛ.

47    Camden, sig. a3ʳ.

48    *Ibid.*, sig. b1ᵛ.

49    *Ibid.*, p. 417.

50    *The Legend of Mary, Queen of Scots* (ed. John Fry, 1810), sig. B1ʳ.

51    "To my Most Especiall good Friend, Sir Peter Manwood, Knight of the Honourable Order of the Bath," prefixed (without pagination) to Knolles's translation of Bodin's *Six Bookes of a Commonweale* (1606). Knolles complained that if those "sitting at the helmes of Commonweales" did not change their policy of keeping secret "the reasons and certaine knowledge of the doings of great Estates," then posterity would be defrauded. According to Marc Friedlaender, *Growth in the Resources for Studies in Earlier English History, 1534–1625* (1943), pp. 190-191, Knolles's com-

plaint apparently did some good, for in the 1610 edition of his *Generall History of the Turkes* there are one hundred fifty pages of new material that brought his subject up to date.

52   *Life of Sir Philip Sidney* (ed. Nowell Smith, 1907), pp. 216-219.

53   *Ibid.*, pp. 174-175.

54   John Stow and Edmund Howes, *The Annales, or Generall Chronicle of England* (1615), sig. 8$^r$. Hereafter cited as "Stow-Howes."

55   *The Collection of the History of England* in *Complete Works*, IV, 78.

56   *Basilikon Doron* in *Political Works of James I* (ed. Charles Howard McIlwain, 1918), p. 40.

57   *Reliquiae Spelmannianae. The Posthumous Works* (1723) in *English Works* (2d ed., 1727), pp. 69-70.

58   *The History of the World*, "Preface" (*Works*, II, lxiii).

59   John Chamberlain, *Letters* (ed. Norman Egbert McClure, 2 vols., 1939), I, 568.

60   *The History of the World*, "Preface" (*Works*, II, xviii–xx).

61   *Ibid.*, II, viii–xvii, xx–xxx.

62   *The Historie of Edward the Second . . . Now Published by the Author thereof, according to the true Original Copie, and purged from those foule Errors and Corruptions, Wherewith that spurious and surreptitious Peece, which lately came forth under the same Tytle, was too much defiled and deformed* (1629), sig. A5$^r$–A5$^v$.

63   *Method for the Easy Comprehension of History*, p. 15.

64   *Advancement of Learning* in *Works*, VI, 183.

65   *The Method and Order of Reading Both Civil and Ecclesiastical Histories* (trans. Edmund Bohun, 1685), p. 16. Hereafter cited as "Wheare."

66   Sidney, *An Apologie for Poetrie* in Smith, I, 152-153.

67   *The History of the World*, "Preface" (*Works*, II, vi).

68   Wheare, p. 361.

69   Bolton, p. 233.

70   *A Survey of History: Or, A Nursery for Gentry* (1638), p. 64.

71   Ludowick Lloyd, *The Consent of Time, Disciphering the errors of the Grecians in their Olympiads*, etc. (1590), sig. a3$^r$, a2$^r$.

72   *Prose Works*, v, 164.

73   *Coopers Chronicle*, sig. h2$^r$.

74   *The History of the World*, II.xxi.6 (*Works*, IV, 612-617).

75   *The Christian Doctrine*, I.xvii (*Prose Works*, IV, 326).

76  See, for example, Raleigh's account of the Greek and Persian wars, *The History of the World*, v.i.3-4 (*Works*, VI, 19-30).
77  *Essays* (Oxford Standard Authors, 1914), pp. 461-463.
78  *The History of the World*, II.xxi.6 (*Works*, IV, 613).
79  II.xix.3 (*Works*, IV, 563).
80  I.vii.10 (*Works*, II, 244).
81  v.iii.9 (*Works*, VI, 284).
82  I.vii.10 (*Works*, II, 244).
83  III.i.13 (*Works*, V, 43); cf. II.i.7 (*Works*, III, 19).
84  III.i.8 (*Works*, V, 27-31).
85  II.xxi.6 (*Works*, IV, 612-617).
86  III.iii.6 (*Works*, V, 70).
87  III.viii.8 (*Works*, V, 179).
88  IV.ii.3 (*Works*, V, 311).
89  *Religio Medici*, I.xix.
90  *The History of the World*, "Preface" (*Works*, II, xlv-xlvii).
91  II.v.10 (*Works*, III, 176-177).
92  I.i.10 (*Works*, III, 176).
93  "Preface" (*Works*, II, lvii); cf. I.i.10 (*Works*, II, 25); II.iii.5 (*Works*, III, 101-102).
94  "Preface" (*Works*, II, xlvii).

## 2 The Use of History

1  *The Annales of England . . . lately corrected, encreased, and continued from the first inhabitation untill this present yeere 1601* (1601), sig. a3ʳ.
2  *The History of the World*, II.xxi.6 (*Works*, IV, 616).
3  Wheare, p. 298.
4  *Plutarch's Lives of the Noble Grecians and Romans Englished by Sir Thomas North* (6 vols., 1895-1896), I, 8.
5  *Ibid.*, I, 10-11.
6  *Ibid.*, I, 7.
7  *An Apologie for Poetrie* in Smith, I, 163.
8  *Coopers Chronicle*, sig. a2ʳ-a2ᵛ.
9  *The Theatre of Gods Iudgements* (1597), p. 471.
10  "A Preface of Simon Grineus to the Reader as concerning the profite of reading Hystories" — i.e. *De utilitate legendae historiae* (1531) – prefixed to Golding's translation of *Thabridgment of the Histories of Trogus Pompeius* (1564). sig. aiʳ. Grynaeus'

popular treatise was also included in Thomas Lodge's translation of Josephus (1602) and in George Wilkins' of Justin (1606).

11    *Plutarch's Lives*, I, 15.

12    *The First Part of the Life and raigne of King Henrie IIII* (1599), sig. A4ʳ.

13    *Life of Sir Philip Sidney*, p. 3.

14    *Thabridgment of the Histories of Trogus Pompeius*, sig. *iiᵛ.

15    *The Acts and Monuments of the Church* (ed. M. Hobart Seymour, 1850?), p. 5. Hereafter cited as "Foxe."

16    *The Arte of English Poesie*, I.xix (Smith, II, 40-41).

17    *The Palace of Pleasure Beautified adorned and well furnished with pleasaunt Histories and excellent Novels* (1575), sig. Viiᵛ–Aiiiʳ.

18    *Certaine Tragicall Discourses written oute of Frenche and Latin* (1567), sig. *iiʳ–*iiᵛ.

19    *The History of the World*, "Preface" (*Works*, II, vi).

20    *Discourses on the First Decade of Titus Livius* (trans. Ninian Hill Thomson, 1883), pp. 5, 125.

21    *The Florentine Histories* (trans. C. Edwards Lester, 2 vols., 1845), I, 15.

22    *Discourses*, II.xiii, IV.xlii.

23    *Religio Medici*, I.xx (ed. James Winny, 1963, p. 25).

24    *Advancement of Learning* in *Works*, VI, 359; cf. VI, 327.

25    *Holinshed's Chronicles*, vol. VI, sig. b4ʳ.

26    Camden, sig. b4ʳ.

27    *The Historie of Tithes*, p. ii.

28    *The three Orations of Demosthenes chiefe Orator among the Grecians* (1570), title page. Perhaps Wilson had in mind the Rising in the North, which had occurred the year before his book was published.

29    *A Discoverie of the True Causes why Ireland was Never entirely Subdued* (1612).

30    *The Historie of Tithes*, sig. a2ʳ–a2ᵛ.

31    *Coopers Chronicle*, sig. g4ʳ. The citation is from Walter Lynne's translation of the preface to Johann Carion's (and perhaps Philip Melanchthon's) *Thre bokes of Cronicles* (1550).

32    "On the Fortunate Memory of Elizabeth Queen of England" in *Works*, XI, 443; Bodin, *Method for the Easy Comprehension of History*, p. 50; cf. Edward Hyde, Earl of Clarendon, *Essays Moral and Entertaining, on the Various Faculties and Passions*

*of the Human Mind* (2 vols., 1815), I, 244.

33  *Essays,* III.viii (trans. E. J. Trechmann, 2 vols., 1935, II, 405).

34  *Mirror,* pp. 65-66.

35  *The three Orations of Demosthenes,* sig. *iiʳ.

36  Dick, pp. 154-155.

37  *Basilikon Doron* in *Political Works of James I,* p. 40.

38  *History of the Reign of King Henry VII* in *Works,* XI, 43.

39  *Clarendon: Selections from The History of the Rebellion and Civil Wars and The Life by Himself* (ed. G. Huehns, The World's Classics, 1955), pp. 6, 1.

40  *Mirror,* pp. 308-309.

41  "Two Cantos of Mutabilitie," viii.2 (*Complete Poetical Works,* ed. R. E. Neil Dodge, The Cambridge Poets, 1908, p. 677).

42  *City of God,* XI.vi, XII.xiv.

43  Browne, *Religio Medici,* I.xi (ed. Winny, p. 13).

44  *Of the Laws of Ecclesiastical Polity,* v.lxix.2 (*Works,* ed. John Keble, 6th ed., 3 vols., 1874, II, 381-382).

45  *Confessions,* XI.xiii (Everyman's Library, 1907, p. 262).

46  *Ibid.,* XI.xviii.

47  *Devotions upon Emergent Occasions* (ed. John Sparrow, 1923), p. 79.

48  George Hakewill, *An Apologie or Declaration of the Power and Providence of God in the Government of the World* (3d ed., 1635), p. 565.

49  XII.553-573.

50  *Religio Medici,* I.xi.

51  *1 Henry IV,* v.iv.82-83.

52  *Sermons of John Donne* (ed. George R. Potter and Evelyn M. Simpson), IV (1959), 162.

53  *City of God,* XXII.xxx.

54  *Coopers Chronicle,* p. 378ʳ; Stow-Howes, p. 948.

55  *Cosmographie,* p. 3.

56  *Sermons* (ed. Potter and Simpson), VII (1954), 138-139.

57  Foxe, p. 32.

58  Stow-Howes, sig. ¶4ʳ– ¶8ʳ.

59  vii:4-7.

60  Johannes Sleiden, *The Key to History* (2d ed., 1631), pp. 372-375.

61  *The General History of the Reformation,* sig. a1ᵛ.

62  Heylin, *Cosmographie,* sig. A6ʳ.

63  *The History of the World,* I.vii.9 (*Works,* I, 187).

64  *Resolves Divine Morall and Politicall* (The Temple Classics 1904), p. 139.

65  *Hydriotaphia*, ch. v (*Religio Medici & Other Writings*, Everyman's Library, 1931, p. 133).

66  i: 4-6.

67  *Statesman*, 269-271 (*Dialogues*, trans. B. Jowett, 2 vols., 1937, II, 297-299).

68  *City of God*, XII.xx (trans. Marcus Dods, The Modern Library, 1950, p. 404).

69  *Ibid.*, XII.xiii (trans. Dods, p. 394).

70  Book VI, pp. 248-249.

71  Book VI, p. 323.

72  *Florentine Histories* II, 6; cf. *Discourses*, p. 125.

73  Page 131.

74  *Method for the Easy Comprehension of History*, p. 291.

75  *Ibid.*, p. 302.

76  Lines 189-190 (*Complete Works*, I, 231).

77  Lines 25-30 (*Complete Works*, III, 100).

78  Lines 348-358 (*Complete Works*, III, 52). For Daniel's application of the cyclic theme to history see *The Collection of the History of England* in *Complete Works*, IV, 85-86.

79  *Prose Works*, V, 393; cf. V, 235.

80  *Religio Medici*, I.xvii (ed. Winny, pp. 21-22).

81  *The Union of the two noble and illustre fameliies of Lancastre & Yorke* (1548), sig. Aj^v.

82  "To the Right Noble Lady, The Lady Marie, Countesse Dowager of Pembroke," *The Civil Wars* (ed. Laurence Michel, 1958), p. 67.

83  *Religio Medici*, I.xvii (ed. Winny, pp. 20-21).

84  *Commentaries* (trans. and ed. Joseph Haroutunian and Louise Pettibone Smith, The Library of Christian Classics, 1958), pp. 266-267; cf. p. 275.

85  I.ii.173-174 (*Complete Plays of Christopher Marlowe*, ed. Irving Ribner, 1963, p. 61); cf. Robert Greene, *The Comicall Historie of Alphonsus King of Arragon*, lines 1481-1482 (*Plays and Poems*, ed. J. Churton Collins, 2 vols., 1905, I, 122).

86  *Plutarch's Lives*, I, 15-16.

87  *A Mask (Comus)*, lines 587-588 (*Complete Poetical Works*, ed. Douglas Bush, 1965, p. 128).

88  *Paradise Lost*, VII.173 (*Complete Poetical Works*, p. 344). In *The*

*Art of Logic,* I.v (Columbia *Milton,* XI, 1935, 49), providence is defined as "the first cause of all things, whether their secondary causes are known or unknown, and if necessity is joined to providence it is usually called fate."

89  *Novum Organum,* Aphorism lx; "Of Fortune," *Essays,* no. xl,
90  *The History of the World,* I.i.ii; cf. *ibid.,* I.i.15; Richard Brathwaithe, *A Survey of History,* sig. A1ᵛ.
91  *Of the Laws of Ecclesiastical Polity,* I.iii.v (*Works,* I, 210).
92  Foxe, p. 32.
93  *The State of Christendom* (1657), p. 7; cf. p. 87 (on the reign of Queen Elizabeth).
94  Ed. William Frederick Poole, 1867, pp. 1-2.
95  *The Theatre of Gods Iudgements,* sig. A3ʳ.
96  *An Apologie,* p. 87.
97  *The Anatomy of Melancholy,* II.ii.3 (ed. A. R. Shilleto, Bohn's Standard Library, 3 vols., 1896, II, 69).
98  *The Divine Catastrophe of the Kingly Family of the House of Stuarts* in *Secret History of the Court of James the First* (ed. Walter Scott, 2 vols., 1811), II, 370-371.
99  *Holinshed's Chronicles,* IV, 81.
100  Bolton, p. 254.

# 3  The Form of History

1  *Mirror,* p. 198.
2  *The Scholemaster* in *English Works,* p. 260.
3  *A Report and Discourse . . . of the affaires and state of Germany* in *English Works,* p. 126.
4  *Pierce Penilesse His Supplication to the Divell* in *Works* (ed. Ronald B. McKerrow, 5 vols., 1904-1910), I, 194; cf. *Summers Last Will and Testament,* McKerrow, III, 276, on "Historiographers" who "for a penny, or a halfe-penny" would write about a cobbler so as to make him sound better than the Black Prince.
5  Foxe, p. 2.
6  "On the Fortunate Memory of Elizabeth, Queen of England" in *Works,* XI, 443.
7  *De Augmentis Scientiarum* in *Works,* VIII, 421-422.
8  *The Collection of the History of England* in *Complete Works,* IV, 75-76.
9  *The Lives of the III. Normans, Kings of England,* sig. A2ʳ-A2ᵛ;

cf. *The First Part of the Life and raigne of King Henrie IIII,* sig. A4ᵛ.

10  Bolton, p. 223.

11  *Ibid.,* p. 237.

12  *Nero Caesar, or Monarchie Depraved,* sig. Qa3ᵛ–Qq4ʳ.

13  *The History of Great Britaine* (1611), p. 598.

14  Quoted by Marc Friedlaender, *Growth in the Resources for Studies in Earlier English History, 1534–1625,* pp. 188-189

15  *History of the Reign of King Henry VII* in *Works,* xi, 35.

16  *The Collection of the History of England* in *Complete Works,* iv, 82.

17  *A Common-place Book* (ed. Alfred J. Horwood, Camden Society, New Series, xvi, 1877, 9, 10, 13, 22, 25, 27, 31; cf. *Of Reformation Touching Church-Discipline in England* (ed. Will Taliaferro Hale, 1916), p. iv; James Holley Hanford, "The Chronology of Milton's Private Studies," *PMLA,* xxxvi (1921), 297, 301.

18  *The Reason of Church Government Urged against Prelaty* in *Prose Works,* ii, 478.

19  *Of Reformation in England* in *Prose Works,* ii, 380.

20  *History of Britain* in *Prose Works,* v, 228.

21  *Ibid.,* v, 295-296.

22  *Familiar Letters,* no. xxiii in *Prose Works,* iii, 515.

23  *History of Britain* in *Prose Works,* v, 186.

24  *Ibid.,* v, 234-235.

25  *Essays Moral and Entertaining,* i, 244, 246, 250-251.

26  *The Civil Wars,* v.iv-v (ed. Michel, p. 179).

27  Book ii, Prologue (*Complete Poetical Works,* p. 230).

28  *The Arte of English Poesie,* i.xix (Smith, ii, 42).

29  *A Refutation of the Apology for Actors . . . By I.G.* (1615), p. 42.

30  "Mansus," lines 80-84; *The Reason of Church Government* in *Prose Works,* ii, 478.

31  *History of Britain* in *Prose Works,* v, 165, 167-168, 173, 175.

32  *Poetics,* 1451a.

33  *De Legibus,* i.i.5.

34  *On the Composition of Romances* in *Literary Criticism: Plato to Dryden* (ed. Allan H. Gilbert, 1940), p. 271.

35  *On the Poetics* in *Literary Criticism,* pp. 305-306.

36  *Discourses on the Heroic Poem* in *Literary Criticism,* pp. 482, 494.

37  *An Apologie for Poetrie* in Smith, i, 156, 164.

38  "A Letter of the Authors . . . to the Right Noble, and Valorous,

Sir Walter Raleigh" in *Complete Poetical Works*, p. 137.

39    *Life of Sir Philip Sidney*, pp. 2-3.

40    *The Tragical Reign of Selimus 1594* (ed. W. Bang, Malone Society Reprints, 1908), sig. A2$^v$; cf. *Henry the Eighth*, "The Prologue."

41    *Works* (ed. A. H. Bullen, 3 vols., 1887), ii, 235.

42    *Dramatic Works* (ed. Fredson Bowers), ii (1955), 497.

43    Sig. A3$^v$.

44    *Method for the Easy Comprehension of History*, p. 55.

45    *Advancement of Learning* in *Works*, vi, 203.

46    "A Preface of Simon Grineus to the Reader as concerning the profite of reading Hystories" in *Thabridgment of the Histories of Trogus Pompeius* (trans. Arthur Golding, 1564), sig. Aii$^r$, Aiii$^r$.

47    *A Report and Discourse . . . of the affaires and state of Germany* in *English Works*, p. 126.

48    See above, p. 29.

49    Camden, sig. b2$^r$.

50    *Holinshed's Chronicles*, "The Preface to the Reader," vol. ii.

51    Stow-Howes, sig. ¶1$^r$.

52    *Thabridgment of the Histories of Trogus Pompeius*, sig. *vii$^v$.

53    *The Romane Historie Written by T. Livius of Padua . . . Translated out of Latine into English, by Philemon Holland, Doctor in Physicke* (1600), "To the Reader."

54    Hobbes, sig. a4$^r$.

55    *The Civil Wars* (ed. Michel), p. 68.

56    *A Survey of History*, p. 30 (misnumbered 32); cf. p. 12, on the intrusion of "frivolous Ambages" into historical narrations.

57    *The General History of the Reformation of the Church*, sig. a2$^v$. In a seventeenth-century translation and abridgement of Sleiden's *De Quatuor Summis Imperiis* (which went through three editions in ten years), the anonymous translater explained that although he himself preferred a "lofty" style, he had dutifully followed Sleiden's "plaine, facile, and methodicall narration." See *The Key to History* (n. 60 to Lecture 2), sig. B3$^r$.

58    Dick, p. 164.

59    *Familiar Letters*, no. xxvi in *Prose Works*, iii, 518; cf. *History of Britain* in *Prose Works*, v, 210-211 (on interpolated speeches).

60    *Familiar Letters*, no. xxiii in *Prose Works*, iii, 515.

61    *Historiae Anglicanae libri XXVI . . . ex nova ed. Antonii Thysii*, (1649), pp. 25-26.

62    *The Cronycles of Englande and of dyvers other realmes* (1636?),
      "Prologus."

63    *A Learned and True Assertion of the original, Life, Actes, and
      death of the most Noble, Valiant, and Renoumed Prince Arthure,
      King of great Britaine* (trans. Richard Robinson, 1582), p. 38$^v$.

64    *The Arte of English Poesie*, i.xix (Smith, ii, 43-44).

65    *Have With You to Saffron-Walden* in *Works* (ed. McKerrow).
      iii, 85.

66    *The Annales of England* (1601), p. 10.

67    Page 474. Munday's account of British history seems to be based
      largely on Henry Lyte's *Light of Britain*, a sumptuous genealogical
      table that was presented to Elizabeth in 1588 and that traced her
      straight descent from Brut. In 1610 Henry Lyte's son Thomas pre-
      pared an updated version of the chart for James I, who expressed
      his gratitude with a miniature (by Nicholas Hilliard) set in dia-
      monds. See Anthony à Wood, *Athenae Oxonienses . . . To Which
      Are Added the Fasti* (ed. Philip Bliss, 5 vols., 1813-1820), ii, 649-
      650.

68    Stow-Howes, sig. ¶2$^r$–¶2$^v$.

69    *Coopers Chronicle*, p. 28$^r$.

70    *Holinshed's Chronicles*, "The Preface to the Reader," vol. ii.

71    *The Collection of the History of England* in *Complete Works*, iv,
      85-86.

72    Bolton, pp. 231, 226.

73    "Illustration" to *Poly-Olbion*, Song ii in *Works of Michael Dray-
      ton* (ed. J. William Hebel), iv (1933), 46-47.

74    "The Beginning of the History of Great Britain" in *Works*, xi,
      406; cf. *De Augmentis Scientiarum* in *Works*, viii, 423–424 on
      "the fabulous accounts of the origins of nations."

75    Wheare, p. 138.

76    *An Apologie*, p. 9.

77    *A Chronicle of the Kings of England*, p. 2.

78    *Cosmographie*, "Of the Ocean and Isles of Britain," p. 257.

79    See above, p. 82.

80    *History of Britain* in *Prose Works*, v, 165; cf. v, 167-168 (on
      Brut), 197, 202 (on Geoffrey of Monmouth), 258-259 (on the
      Arthurian material).

81    *Ibid.*, v, 175.

82    *Ibid.*, v, 184.

This book has been set in Linotype Palatino, with Optima display, and printed by offset on Warren's Olde Style stock by Edwards Brothers, Ann Arbor, Michigan. The binding cloths are Bancroft's Arrestox and Kennett.

DESIGN: Laurie Lewis